MW01233100

Johnny Hoosier

Lessons Learned in the Heartland

by

Harrison Hunt

Bloomington, IN

Milton Keynes, UK

AuthorHouse™
1663 Liberty Drive, Suite 200
Bloomington, IN 47403
www.authorhouse.com
Phone: 1-800-839-8640

AuthorHouse™ UK Ltd.
500 Avebury Boulevard
Central Milton Keynes, MK9 2BE
www.authorhouse.co.uk
Phone: 08001974150

First published by AuthorHouse 5/1/2007

ISBN: 978-1-4343-0901-3 (sc)
ISBN: 978-1-4343-0900-6 (hc)

Library of Congress Control Number: 2007903142

Printed in the United States of America
Bloomington, Indiana

This book is printed on acid-free paper.

Contents

Chapter One

The Segue

"That's an ominous looking cloud moving in from the West" I said to my new friend and fishing buddy, Gib Taylor. Gib didn't respond other than shrug his shoulders and grunt as if to say, " so".

We had been out on Dale Hollow Lake in my I/O open bow runabout for nearly four hours and I was looking for any reason to head back to shore and some lunch. "Johnny", Gib finally said, "if you want to wrap up we can head in, we really haven't been hitting today." I had only a nibble or two and Gib, the fisherman that he was, wasn't about to do anything other than return his three small catches back to the water.

As we headed back to the marina and our boat slip, the wind suddenly whipped up and we faced what seemed to be endless white caps in open water. The water was getting pretty rough. Getting back to Star Point Marina was taking our undivided attention and we missed our normal enjoyment of soaking in the beauty of the shoreline with it's shale cliffs, endless mountains, tree covered with a variety of species including our favorite, the multitude of southern pine and glorious deciduous trees that soon would give us the aura of rainbow colors. We were prejudiced of course, as were most of the local residents. We even delighted in the suffrutescent samplings struggling for their place in the vegetation. We were happy, of course, when we reached the shallows near the marina with it's buoys and crystal clear water.

"Well Johnny, where do you want to eat?" Gib asked. "We can go to the buffet at the Farm House Restaurant, the Bobcat Den on Route 111, or the Dixie Café. You realize, of course, that the Dixie will not have Bluegrass music since it is not Friday or Saturday evening." "No", I said, "let's go up on the hill by Sunset Marina to Moogy's." That settled it, we were going to Moogy's where Gib could have his fill of catfish and I would dine on my staple, ground sirloin and a baked potato.

Gib was an interesting guy with a very successful career behind him. He had his bachelor's degree from Tennessee Tech University and his graduate degree, with distinction, from Ball State University. His children include a medical doctor and an international petroleum executive. So he was also successful at parenting. Although widowed now for some time, he was active in local affairs including a community theater group and the local Chamber of Commerce. An extroverted and outgoing guy, he had befriended me and my wife Paula, at the Dixie Cafe the night after we closed on our retirement home out by Star Point Marina. Gib has frequently reminded me of a favorite of his that he has followed to this day. Gib says, "if you talk nice to people, you get the nicest people to talk to you". Pretty good coaching, eh?

Other than our realtors, Jim and Patti Pyzik , he was our first local contact. We had located and contacted Jim and Patti on the Internet from our home on the Gulf Coast in Florida. Both Paula and I were immediately struck by the lack of pretensions and the open friendly atmosphere by folks around Dale Hollow Lake. Even though we had lived in Indianapolis, the Twin Cities in Minnesota, New York and the Gulf Coast of Florida previously, the quiet friendly nature of things seemed just right for our stage in life. There simply was no such thing as being ostentatious. Newcomers from as far away as California and Florida were quickly assimilating into the way of life in Northern Tennessee. Gib had been in the insurance business and was a corporate trainer in Indianapolis. He was now into local politics and was an aspiring author. I liked him a lot. He was one given to sage counsel no doubt.

After we ordered, Gib remarked that he had not seen the water level in the lake as low as it now was. I asked if that might be connected to the repair work that was now being done on the dam up stream from Star Point Marina. Gib agreed that could have an impact but even so the water level was extremely low.

Gib then turned to his writing efforts and said that he was in the middle of research for what he hoped would be a novel that would hit the New York Times best sellers list. Suddenly, Gib said, "Johnny, you know, you lived in a number of places in your career in business, why don't you tell me about some of your experiences." Dumfounded, I retorted, "Gib my business life, although quite successful, was not particularly remarkable but I could perhaps give you some of my experiences when I grew up in and around Muncie, Indiana. You know they wrote a couple of books about the town , "Middletown" and Middletown Revisited"; sociological studies. Gib was interested and I thought to myself "what have I gotten myself into now?" Gib said, "Johnny, start as early as you can and then see how far you can get. Be chronological as much as you can."

So, that is how this story had its genesis.

Chapter Two

Middletown and Middletown Revisited

Middletown and Middletown Revisited with full credits to Robert S. Lynd and Helen Merrell Lynd and Dwight Hoover

Muncie, Indiana, and surrounding Delaware County is much like numerous other communities in our Midwest. The County has seen boom times and periods of retraction and recession. It was a small agricultural community in 1886 when natural gas was discovered which brought about a remarkable transformation into a, albeit small, manufacturing city.

This was an area that had its first permanent settlement in 1820 and its first county government in 1827.

Early on in the 19th century many interesting wives tales abounded. Such as putting a pan of water under your bed to check night sweats, or that bleeding cured the fits, loss of consciousness, fever and other ills. The best cure for fevers was thought to be drinking nanny tea or tea made for sheep dung. And finally, hogs must be slaughtered at certain times of the moon or the bacon would shrink.

The discovery of natural gas twelve miles north of the city was quite by accident. Not unlike perhaps many other noteworthy discoveries over the years. A company was boring for coal and after boring some

600 feet down they only had struck a very foul odor coming from the bowels of the earth. Not knowing what they had struck the discovery lay dormant for another decade when others were to discover natural gas. The boom was then on as a major migration occurred to the area and the manufacturing companies came for this cheap and abundant source of energy. The population doubled and over forty factories arrived.

Then, as abruptly as the natural gas came, it was gone. By the beginning of the twentieth century the population was about 20,000 and the industrial foundation was ready to carry the agricultural area forward.

As the area developed, residents would soon turn their focus to the local high school in town, Muncie Central. Locals would soon view their own self worth by how well the athletic teams were doing and would establish a social life around Friday night basketball and those Bearcats.

The most accomplished successful professional could direct his offspring in the right or wrong thing to do in a given situation, but found he had absolutely no authority when it came to those Friday night athletic contests. It was the members of the Bearcat teams that had control over his children. At least until the athletic contest was over.

High school basketball in the state of Indiana is the paramount social event of every week during the season which is normally from November until late March. Even during the off season, members of an outstanding team were, and are, given undue stature. The dominance of basketball is all-pervasive and during the state tournament many delirious residents abound. One resident is reported to have asked if it would be right to pray for the Bearcats to win. The response, not surprising, is that it would be unsportsmanlike for God to favor the other team. Needless to note, basketball was the center of civic loyalty with all economic levels driving an array of dissimilar vehicles to those away games.

As Eastern Indiana Normal School started its transition to what is now Ball State University, a major university, the school had its early impact on Muncie and surrounding area where public lectures, music recitals and paintings brought a touch of culture to the area. Muncie Burris Laboratory School was opened in 1929 as part of the college. It is interesting that teachers were wrestling verbally back then with school administrators, as they continue to do today, over the size of classes. The issue of pedagogical royalty arose as only those with an M.A. degree were allowed to teach at Burris.

At this time the citizenry in Muncie operated with the belief that the acquisition of money was their paramount goal. The social utility of your work was measured by how much you earned. Businessmen spent long hours earning their social status leaving little time for leisure and recreation. My, my, how times have changed. Some have called this a masochistic tendency which was built into this community. Most people were of the working class, however, and they measured their status in what kind of vehicle they drove. Some probably still do. With this mindset, little was available for saving and investing for the future. So, upward mobility was not an option in the minds of most working class folks.

While nearly 80% of the populace were fans of country and western or popular music, one local entrepreneur, Don Burton, garnered the local radio market by broadcasting the Bearcat games. That status is retained to this day even with all the changes in the sources of music and the multiplicity of mediums of broadcast today.

A couple of other events of the time give credence to how folks felt about their Bearcats. After the Bearcats won their first state high school basketball championship in 1928, and repeated this feat in 1931, each member of the 1931 team received gold watches even though this was the economic depression, the severest know to humankind. The other was that during the late 1920's, when local leaders proceeded to build Muncie Field House which at that time seated some 9,000 spectators.

In the 1950's capacity had been reduced to some 7,500 because of fire codes. It is even less today. The builders, who were local business chaps, incurred an obligation of some $347,000, an enormous sum at that time. It was to be paid over a fourteen year period. During the depression, which followed shortly, this became somewhat of a white elephant and was used for junior high school classes despite its unfitness for this use.

In fully understanding the State of Indiana and its athletic traditions here are some of its most recognized personalities.............George McGinnis, Larry Bird, Tommy John, Oscar Robertson, Tony Hinkle, John Pont, Jack Mollenkopf, Carl Erskine, Branch McCracken, Knute Rockne (although he was originally for Minnesota), John Wooden and Mr. Bearcat himself Ron Bonham. Other names which may be of interest include John Dillinger, Hoagy Carmichael, Billy Sunday, the KKK, Eugene Debs, Colonel Eli Lilly, James Dean and Carol Lombard. If your favorite isn't mentioned here it was not intentional.

As I caught my breadth, Gib, an amateur historian himself, said he was fascinated with what I related but wanted to know about any other area in Indiana to which I could make reference. As I stammered and sought for a congruent thought, it came to me that my father-in-law, Jim Bright, who had grown up in the Waldron area (Brown County) and Greensburg area, would be a perfect choice.

Chapter Three

Jim Bright, What it was Like in the 1940's

Jim, my father-in-law, is gifted in many ways. Handsome even in his seventies today, he still retains that keen and dry wit for which he was, and is, known. Not only was he golf champion a number of times, at his local country club, after he retired at age 50, he is a very bright mind and he built a very successful tool and die company prior to moving to Florida in retirement. My golf game is so shameful as compared to Jim's, there just weren't that many invitations. I understand that. What's a 13 handicap compared to a scratch golfer? Jim was always long and straight and I was only long.

So I started.

Jim grew up in the forties which was a time that tested the sanity of our civilization with the Second World War. For most of us, just barely out of diapers, things of major significance were happening in the world without any immediate impact on us and without us even knowing that they were happening. The words Allies and Axis powers were foreign to us. Nonetheless, leaders such as FDR, Churchill, Truman, Eisenhower and on the dark side, Hitler and Mussolini, were in position to set the stage for our adolescence without war and in an economic environment in which we would not know a lot about the great depression except through our parents. Jim Bright knew a lot about this time and served his country just as this despicable and deadly chapter came to a close. It is people like Jim that my generation owes a great deal of gratitude.

Jim's was a typical small town and was one of a rural nature. There were crossroads in the center of town, with a single stop light. Waldron had a population of less than 1000 people with the great majority of area residents living on farms surrounding the town. It had a quaint aura and had about a block of stores and other places of businesses with a barber shop, a hardware store, an ice cream store or confectionary with a soda fountain and juke box, where you could get 6 plays for a quarter.

It had a second hand store, and what was normally the business focus, a general store. Jim worked in the general store part time, and did chores such as bagging one and five pound bags of sugar and flour, and counting eggs and putting them into cartons, that farmers brought in for credit to their accounts. A railroad ran through the town but the trains seldom stopped. Mail pickup was by an arm attached to the train that would pick off the mailbag from a stationary holding mechanism as the train continued to travel. Mail arrival was by engineering armature, which is that the engineer would simply toss the arriving mail out by arm, his arm, without ever slowing the speed of the train. No home delivery existed. You had to pick your mail up at the post office where you had your own box number.

Jim's schools were very small. As was typical, there was a one or two room school along with a high school. Progressive areas built larger schools with twelve grades under one roof. That was the case in which, I, Johnny Hoosier, and all the other Johnny Hoosiers, would receive all our pre-college education. No kindergartens existed back then let alone pre-school centers. Most kids traveled to school by yellow bus. If you were out and became hungry you simply hopped the closest fence for an apple, pear or a tomato from the vegetable garden of one of your neighbors.

Boys entertained themselves by playing mumblety-peg (a game played with pocket knives). Everyone knew everyone else and helping a neighbor or friend was an everyday occurrence. Most boys grew up to be very successful business men or became the latest edition of a gentleman farmer. Jim Bright is an example of a successful businessman that came for this background.

Jim recanted to me some of his experiences of this time. Jim notes that it was a time of pennies, not dollars. Most candy bars were a penny with the nickel bars being too large for your pockets. If you got an allowance, did your chores such as bringing in the coal for the stove and removing the ashes, and any other assignment from your parents, you got your 25 cents. Money could also be earned by hand hoeing field corn for the local farmers; you could earn 15 cents per row, for each row of a typically sized field, which took an hour.

Bicycles, sling shots and bee bee guns were a sign of the times during the forties. The round symmetrical rocks found along railroad tracks were the best ammunition for the sling shots. Mostly, the sling shots were used to ferret out the pest population. On other occasions, you could shoot holes in your hat which was primarily used by all the boys for sun protection. Jim told me of two of his buddies, who were twins and the most expert with the sling shot, putting two holes in his hat before it could come back down after being thrown in the air. What an explanation that must have been when Jim told his parents how two holes were put into his only hat.

Jim tells of the swimming hole he and his friends had at Conn's Creek. It was known as the "16" by all but was now only about six feet deep. Skinny dipping was in for the boys with the girls sneaking up to get a peek. Scouting was a major thing for the boys. And, Jim and a close friend tried camping out a couple of times. The first time, after setting up camp and cooking their meal, the two young boys settled into their tent and told each other ghost stories for entertainment.

Finally finished, they settled in for the night when a cow came up to their tent and let out the loudest moo you've ever heard. It scared the two so badly that they ran all the way to a relative's house. The two boys tried the tent idea out once more and, unfortunately, it rained so hard they were soaked. That was their last tent attempt. Nonetheless, Boy Scouts was a big thing at the time. It was still around in the fifties although scouting suffered from the competition of other activities for young boys.

The forties was a time that was the best and worst of times. It was a conundrum of unfathomable proportions for those living at the time. Money was tight and there just was no spare cash, but friends were abundant and lasted a lifetime. Surviving included using a hand crank to separate the cream in your milk that you derived from your family's own brown swiss or other milk cows.

You used to "cry" unabashedly when hand grinding the horse radish for your mother. Your meat was derived from slaughtering a hog and calf each fall.

All these were the foundation for well learned lessons as this generation matured to adulthood.

An uncle of Jim's bolted a piece of 4X4 to the clutch pedal of their pickup truck to allow Jim to fully engage the clutch since he was not very tall at the time. Jim would later grow to an adult height well in excess of six feet tall. After doing this, his uncle announced that he was going to make Jim a farmer. There was a commonly known saying at the time that "if you had a son you had a hired hand and if you had two sons you had one-half of a hired hand and if you had three or more sons you had no help." Perhaps some things never change. Boys just have to play! Jim wasn't interested in farming and would become a very successful businessman in the tool and die business owning his own business for a number of years selling it, at about age 50, for retirement.

Most family homes were just beginning to get indoor running water and bath rooms at this time. Every home seemed to have an outhouse with a half moon carved in the door. Some of Jim's friends and he would frequently head to the "16" hole where they would wash with a bar of Ivory soap since it would float. This was the preferred method since washing in the rain barrel was most difficult. Most boys began to notice that the girls were beginning to dress differently and to put stuff on their faces. Adulthood was not far off.

Sometime about 1947-48, almost all the schools that had not previously done so were building larger schools that included all twelve grades. The one and two roomers were being torn down.

One of the better known athletes of the time was Marvin Woods from Morristown who later went on to coach Bobby Plump at Milan when they became state basketball champions. They would defeat Oscar Robertson, the NBA Hall of Famer from Indianapolis Crispus Attucks as well as Muncie Central in the championship game. The score was 32 to 30 with Plump hitting the winning jumper as time expired not giving the Bearcats an opportunity to respond.

Most schools had a basketball team, a softball team, which would later become baseball, and a track and field team. Each game would be a major social outing in the community and would be sold out. These phenomena would continue until well into the 1960's and beyond. Jim tells of a game during his junior year being played in a rather compact gymnasium. The court was laid out, of necessity, with the out of bounds lines against the walls. In order to cross as a spectator you walked across the playing court when the game was being contested at the other end of the court.

One of Jim's team mates intercepted an opponent's pass and drove to the other end for a lay up. Jim, in following the play for a potentially needed tip in of his teammate's miss, suddenly ran into some high school girls walking across the floor with soft drinks in paper cups, spilling the drinks all over him. He thought he was hit with a hammer and noted that the drinks were "ice cold". Then he noted that his buddy made the basket and he didn't need to get so wet after all.

Jim notes with some reverence, another outstanding athlete at the time was Bill Garrett from Shelbyville who were state basketball champions in 1947. Bill would go on to star at Indiana University and then head up the AAU for several years. Jim also played against Clyde Lovellette of Terre Haute Garfield, who would go on to star in college at the University of Kansas and the NBA.

If a youngster wanted his first car, which was a major thrill that would continue for years, he could hire on with a local farmer or work pumping gas at the local service station or even work at the local drive in restaurant if his town was large enough to have one. Jim tells of working for a dairy farmer where he would arrive early on Monday morning prior to the morning milking and stay until after the milking was completed on Saturday evening. Some weekend.

Getting that first car was also a high risk, at least until new models came on the market following the retooling that manufacturers went through following the war, since getting an older model with an out of round crankshaft was not unusual. These problems didn't seem to detract from this once in a lifetime experience, however.

Entertainment for youngsters in the 1940's included hayrides and taffy pulls. Waldron had a youth hangout joint where you found a jukebox, ice cream and soda fountain, etc. Football players played both offense and defense and the boys usually sat out the sock hops and the girls danced.

Jim noted that during these times you learned to carry your load and developed pride in being a Hoosier.

"Quite a background for starting our travel through the 1950's", I remarked to Gil. He agreed and wanted to get on with it.

Chapter Four

Prelude to the 1950's at Harrison Township High School

"Gib" I said, "in order to more fully understand where Johnny Hoosier came from, let me relate a little about the 1930's at Harrison Township High School which was built in 1924, and some of the things that I think will help transcend this period and get us to the action of the 1950's. I want to tell you about Harrison's County Championships of 1930 and 1931 and the Yeager Brothers and my Coach Boggs who was part of the championship teams at Selma High School during the 1940's." Gib was all ears. That was all the encouragement that I needed.

The Yeager Brothers and 1930 and 1931

One year after the first Delaware County high school basketball tournament, a team from Harrison Township would bring the first of two successive championships to HHS. At this time basketball was the only well organized sport for high schoolers in Delaware County. Baseball was still being developed as a secondary school activity. Only a game or two were played since the boys were all busy on family farms during the summer season. It was later that school leaders discovered that a fall baseball season was possible after everyone returned to school in the fall.

In 1930, led by two sophomore brothers, Jim and Bill Yeager and outstanding guard Bob Couden, the Cardinals would prevail over Yorktown in the final game by a score of 27 to 23. In reaching the finals, Harrison had the better of Selma, Daleville and Gaston. The last two games against Daleville and Gaston were close games with the Cards winning by two over the Bronchos and by four over the Bulldogs.

As reported by the local daily newspaper at the time, "The feature game of the opening round saw Harrison Township's netters, undefeated this season, rally and to win their tenth consecutive victory, 31 to 19, at the expense of the plucky Selma Blue Birds." And further, "Harrison's uncanny ability to connect with the nets from every position and angle told the story. Yeager(Jim), whose work has been a feature of Harrison's victory march this season, counted six times from the floor and only one marker, that in the closing minutes was really earned. He seized the ball from the tip off and dribbled through the entire Selma defense for an easy one."

On Sunday, following the tournament, The Muncie Star, described the Cardinals this way. "Harrison, a team which made no pretense at playing brilliant, scientific basketball, but which possessed that much-to-be desired knack of snagging baskets whenever the occasion demands it, whipped the polished Tiger aggregation, not because of superior basketball, but because of a supply of fighting spirit that swept all before it. When the Harrison outfit was far behind, as it was most of the time, it never for a moment lost its head, and always produced the necessary punch in the pinches."

"Yeager, the sensational Cardinal forward, was the most deadly scorer which (sic) has played on the Muncie floor this year. With two and often three players guarding him, he continued to snag his marvelous field goals, shooting from the most difficult of positions".

In an article from the same daily publication, Ken Waite describes his take on the tournament this way. "The truly comeback kids took honors in the second annual Delaware County tourney during the week-end. In every game, these Harrison Township High School representatives in the game of tossing the leather sphere through the little iron hoop came from behind to continue their undefeated record so far this season. Their first decision came at the expense of the Selma Blue Birds, 31 to 19; their second from the Daleville five, 23 to 21, in an overtime game; their third from the Gaston Bulldogs, 34 to 30, and their fourth from the Yorktown Tigers, one of the best working combinations entered, 27 to 23, after each opponent had grabbed an early lead and held the advantage until sometimes late in the game. Yes, they truly are the comeback kids."

"Two predominating qualities in the Harrison's team's play were its coolness under fire and its uncanny ability to snag baskets from every any place on the floor and from any angle. These, of course, made possible its comeback drives."

"After the tourney, one coach asked this question, 'How long can they keep it up?' in referring to the Kigermen's (referring to Coach Francis Kiger) ability to connect with the basket. They have been doing that all year and we'd say it is probable they will continue. It's just a habit with them now."

In retrospect, and complete honestly, I only wish that the 1958 Cardinals (eleven wins and no losses prior to the tournament) could have had that kind of tenacity. At least Johnny Hoosier would not have been haunted all these years by the loss to Royerton in the tournament. But then, what a life's lesson that was.

Actually, Bill Yeager was a year younger than his brother Jim although both were sophomores, Jim, actually eleven months Bill's senior, refused to start school until his Brother Bill could go with him. So the Yeager brothers graduated in the same class. They started their academic careers in the old Bethel School, a two story affair at that time, and continued there until the new Harrison School was built in 1924.

During the 1930 season, Jim was a regular while Bill was not. The starters on this championship team, at least in the final game against Yorktown, were Jim Yeager, Harvey Johnson, Gerald Melvin, Bob Couden and Gene McCreery. Yeager, Melvin and Couden were selected to the all tournament team.

In 1931 the Cardinals repeated as champions, beating Cowan by ten points in the final game. All tournament selections included both Jim and Bill Yeager, and Bob Couden. Couden and Jim Yeager were repeat selections from the year before. Harvey Johnson was again back in the pivot position with these three with all being joined by Fred Johnson at guard. The Cards soundly thumped all their opponents this time around beating Albany by 17 points, Yorktown by fifteen and finally Cowan by ten in the final game. We must remind ourselves that these were remarkable scores since wholesale scoring was yet to come to the high school game. The winners had averaged only 26.6 points per game, losers 18.5 points per game during this tournament. Of course, the rules were different then, with a center jump after each score, etc. Even so, the margins of victory were exceptional.

As the Cardinals and the Yeager Brothers approached the tournament as seniors in 1932, confidence abounded. Alas, it was not to be. The Cards were ousted by a single point by the Center Spartans who would be the eventual champions over a tough team from Royerton , again, by a single point. That game ended with Center, the champs having scored only four field goals and three free throws and the Redbirds also scoring four field goals but only a pair of free throws. Bob Couden was the only Card to be selected to the all tournament team. Jim Rodeffer from Center would be selected all tournament after failing to score in the championship game. The Cardinals would go on to be ousted in the Sectional Tournament by Muncie Central by four points.

The headlines following Harrison's ouster by the Bearcats in the 1932 Sectional went like this, "Bearcats have a real struggle with Harrison" Having lost in the county tournament by a single point to the eventual winner, the Cardinals were once again a formidable group.

The March 5, 1932, Muncie Star had this to say about this Cardinal-Bearcat encounter. "The Muncie-Harrison combat was the thriller of the opening day. The Cardinals played a splendid game, presenting a defense that had the Bearcats stopped cold on several occasions and manifested an ability to hit from out on the floor that made the situation look serious on several occasions." The scores by quarter breaks went like this: 1st quarter, Cardinals 6, Bearcats 0; 2nd quarter, Bearcats 13, Cardinals 6, 3rd quarter, Bearcats 16, Cardinals 14 and the final, Bearcats 24, Cardinals 20. Actually the score stood at 22 to 20 in favor of the Bearcats until a tip in at the final buzzer. What a game this had been. Ever wonder what it would have been if the Bearcats had not played on their home court. Scoring for the Cardinals was very well balanced with Bill Yeager scoring 8 points, Jim Yeager and Buford Rathel scoring 4 points a piece and Spangler and Bob Couden chipping in with 2 a piece.

There would not be a Cardinal outfit comparable to this group until the later part of the 1950's in my view although the early 1950's group with Larry Campbell and Del Painter were certainly close.

The Yeager eighth grade team was known to have beaten some high school teams back then when they apparently were allowed to engage in such athletic contests. I am not sure when that practice ceased but I know there is a great disparity in the development of eighth grade boys and those as much as four years their senior. After high school, the Yeager's played for King's Chapel Church where they were to become know as the "terrible Yeager boys" since they frequently beat teams made up of former Bearcats from Muncie Central.

Later on, after having graduated, and still living in the Muncie area, I recall an undefeated season with Olive Chapel Church in the local church league. We were both seasonal and tournament champions. We played a number of former Bearcats as the Yeager Brothers had done earlier. I recall that two of my former high school teammates, Bill Long and Phil Glaze were stellar members of that group. We were led by Coach Freddie Niccum, another Harrison alumni member. This would be my last effort in organized basketball as other priorities took my focus.

A boyhood friend of the Yeager brothers, Garland Click, now a ninety-two year old hospital volunteer, who to this day is very clear in his communications and has a wealth of humor. Garland says that he even learned to ride on Jim Yeager's bicycle. They were close and only lived a fraction of a mile from each other. Both the Click's and Yeager's lived a couple of miles west of the Harrison school building on the same E/W road that we called the Harrison-Royerton Road in the 1950's.

The Yeager's had electricity and modern plumbing while most others did not at that time. Electricity was powered by a Delco System as rural electrification would come later. The Yeager parents were farmers. During the depression residents burned corn rather than coal since corn was only a few cents per bushel.

Garland says the Yeager brothers got along well together since their Mother "kept'um straight". Once when a small group of boys were out doing their thing, it was suggested that they throw rocks at some nearby windows. Jim Yeager, in his leadership style, simply said "NO". And that was the end of that bad idea. The boys are known to have smoked corn silks though. That's a far cry from things you hear today about athletes of all ages. I am sure you agree. Earning money was from shoveling corn and picking tomatoes. Sounds like the things that our influx of illegals do today since we simply won't do those things and without getting into the supply/demand curve for labor and its impact on prevailing wages..

Jim Yeager actually hauled gravel as a junior and senior and then bought himself a 1927 Ford. Jim would drive that Ford around and pick up 3 or 4 boys and then they were off. Not too fast mind you, since the top speed was around 35 mph. The boys did have at least one exciting incident. As they approached a T-intersection with a post seemingly in the middle of the road, they were lucky to have made the turn. That makes me speculate what would have happened at the speeds of today.

Garland says that Jim would 'deal' a lot with the girls from Alexandria while Bill was known to see some girls from Daleville. However, both would marry Harrison girls, Jim to Sara Jane Johnson and Bill would marry Helen Finley. Both went on to raise outstanding children. Jim's son Larry went on to star for four years for Muncie Burris in the 1950's. Bill fathered two girls, Joyce the wife of my team mate and optometrist Tom Robbins, and Judy the spouse of handsome Bob Campbell. Jim went on to mechanics school and then worked for Delco Battery. Bill would work for Owens-Illinois in their glass manufacturing operation.

In researching for this writing effort, Judy arranged for me to meet with her Mother, Helen Finley Yeager. A diminutive, attractive and articulate young lady of some 89 summers, she let me in on some of the secrets of the Yeager boys. She says that during the basketball season the boys could not date. Well, we had something not removed from that a great deal with Coach Boggs. Looking back, they were doing the right thing. They were just trying to protect their investment in us players although at the time it certainly didn't seem to make a lot of sense. After all, we were very young minds at the time.

Helen reminded me of the way of life back then as everyone raised most everything in their vegetable gardens and had their own meat. You canned the garden produce and even buried apples and turnips in a mound which you made in the garden. Baseball was played with the neighbor kids and the "boys" would open the corner door in their home and shoot over it. I emphasize that this was in the house. This must have made some racket. This is similar to what we did in our bedroom when we used a pair of rolled up socks and shot over the curtain rods covering our windows. Jim, the elder brother, bought a new car with a rumble seat. Yes, I know what that is. She didn't say that was where she and Bill spent some quality time. It must have been a hoot since everyone wanted to ride in that rumble seat. After graduation, the kids as new graduates, went downtown and simply window shopped. This was not the mall, I repeat, it was not the mall, it was downtown.

Helen says that both Yeager boys were the quiet ones. While Bill was 5'11", Jim was a mere 5'6". Jim was elected to the Delaware County Athletic Hall of Fame in 1980, some fifty odd years after the championships of 1930 and 1931. Bill and Helen would live a marvelous married life for just a week short of their 60th wedding anniversary when Bill passed away on 3-27-97.

She remembers Bill as the one who always knew how to get anywhere and frequently Sunday afternoons were spent driving here and there on family outings. The only dichotomy seems to be during the 1960's when Bill was attempting to find the New York World's Fair he ended up following a car into a Jewish cemetery. So, Helen, my dear, help me on this one please.

Bethel School, Number Six

Harrison High School 1924-1967

Harrison Cardinals County Champions 1930
Front row L to R: Gene McCreery, Jim Yeager. Row two L to R: Ervin Spangler, Bill Yeager, Garnet Dunn, Hamilton Jackson. Row three L to R: Bob Couden, Gerald Melvin, Coach Francis Kiger, Harvey Johnson, Buford Rathel

Harrison Cardinals County Champions 1931
Front row L to R: Jim Yeager, Cletis Gillespie. Row two L to R: Garnet Dunn, Fred Johnson, Buford Rathel, Bill Yeager. Third row L to R: Ervin Spangler, Harvey Johnson, Coach Francis Kiger, Lawrence Taylor, Bob Couden

Photographs furnished courtesy of the Star Press

Chapter Five

Gene McCreery

Another member of the 1930 champions was none other than Gene McCreery. Gene has had an outstanding career all over the globe but rushes to add that I was only the sixth man on that team. He is another self-effacing gentleman. He is now some 94 summers past his birth date, but still walks in a pace that borders on jogging. His class of 1930 had 33 members as seventh graders with 16 graduating.

Gene went to the old Bethel school with the Yeagers and Garland Click, and then attended Gaston for four years, going by horse and buggy with friend Bill Markle. Gene's role model was his father, a teacher who taught at a number of schools including Harrison Township and was still teaching even at age 80.He also was know to have shoveled oats into storage at age 75. His Dad would bring home library books for Gene every two weeks. That's where he got his joy of reading and learning.

Insofar as basketball went, Gene says they started their team as fifth graders and by the time they were in the eighth grade could whip most high school teams. In some states, even today, eighth graders are permitted to play varsity ball. Should have let these guys loose much earlier, huh? During Gene's final year in 1930, he says they lost to Daleville once and then to Alexandria. There were no other blemishes on their record except, of course, in the sectional. They used to do the figure eight weave on offense which worked well for them. We even did that a few times with Coach Boggs. Gene notes that he was able to get the tying basket against Yorktown in the county championship game when they won 27-23. As a sign of future athletes, the boys used to play on a court constructed in a barn loft with fellows from Gaston and Yorktown joining in many times. The Boggs boys would do this while out at Royerton and we did it on the court John Mills' father and uncle put together for us on Bethel Pike.

Admitting he was a good student in high school, Gene says the brightest student was Fred Orcutt, father of classmate Linda Orcutt, who passed at an early age after building a successful construction business. Gene would enroll at Ball State University after graduation. Not only did he receive has bachelor's degree from BSU, but he also met his wife of several decades, Mary Jane Robbins from Bluffton, Indiana. They would have a son, Richard, now a medical doctor practicing in Colorado, and a second son, John, an architect now in Ohio.

Not only did Gene earn his first sheep skin from Ball state, he went on to earn a Masters Degree in Education from Columbia University in New York City, and a doctorate from Indiana University. Not bad for a country boy from Harrison Township.

Gene would travel to Egypt with the US State Department in their Program in Education for Developing Countries. He would also travel abroad with programs for Southern Illinois University and the University of Utah. Earlier in Gene's career in education, he would teach both at Burris High School and Ball State University. If it had not been for the depression, Gene may very well not have pursued his career in education since he had to renew his license after letting it drop for agrarian interests. Gene taught for at least 48 years. I think he is still teaching us.

Gene says he is most proud of "pleasing my dad". While teaching at Gaston, Gene names these students who have distinguished themselves in the real world. Dean Call, attorney; Ned Tudor, a manager for Marsh Supermarkets; Joe Bartow, an AT&T executive who won one of the top honors in the state math contest; Elmer Kliplinger, who worked for the AEC/TVA; and Don Love, after teaching became a construction millionaire in Texas.

Asked what he would change about today's educational system, Gene quickly mentioned he would install more discipline in today's schools. "Not corporal disciple, but we must have more discipline in our schools."

Wow! Anyone who is not proud that Gene heralds from our territory simply is not up to speed.

Gene McCreery, November 16,2006

Photograph furnished courtesy of the Star Press

Chapter Six

The 1940's—Coach Boggs and the Selma Championships

During the mid-1940's a couple of brothers by the name of Boggs were the best that Delaware County had to offer in high school basketball. Bob, the older of the two, would have a major influence on me, Johnny Hoosier, in my athletic fortunes. As it turned out he came to coach at Harrison Township when I was in the seventh grade and my brother John was a freshman. He would remain at Harrison until the completion of my junior year in high school. I could never understand why Coach Boggs would leave Harrison Township that year. When I recently asked him about this he simply said that some parent had complained and he just went to Selma, which in the long run, was probably a good move.

I tell you what, if someone would identify that parent they would have a buzz saw confronting them. That is simply idealistic selfish behavior by someone who is supposed to be an adult. But then, the township trustee should not kowtow to pressure and allow it to affect a very important decision. This seems somewhat similar to the spin doctors of today when they manipulate the American public in their "news broadcasts".

Of course, the print media has been guilty of this for years in their efforts to win advertising dollars. I know this from over twenty years in the print media. It seems to me, that if you are entrusted with the public trust and have direct or indirect power it must be used wisely and judiciously in a balanced manner.

Coach Boggs had so much to do with our knowledge of the game and our development that it seemed unreasonable that he should leave as we approached our senior year when we were poised to be a powerhouse in the county.

Coach was a seemingly quiet but confident young man, who never raised his voice even as we budding athletes did something immature or not very smart. He was a master of the zone defense. I recall how he painstakingly walked us varsity guys through the alignment of the 1-2-2 zone, never failing to keep a point man always chasing the ball as we rotated from center to side and back again. It served us well as we were to be beaten only by Muncie Central in the finals of the Sectional tournament long before our enrollment of only 122 female and male students in the top four grades would allow us to compete against only those schools of a comparable size. We only had 502 students in our entire twelve grades. This was 1954, when the Milan Indians and Bobby Plump were to put a halt to the talk of developing a tournament that would be divided into classes by enrollment size.

Much later on classes by enrollment size would come to pass and raise outraged cries from the traditionalists. Incidentally, Muncie Central had roughly 1200 students in the top three grades that year. And, of course, we played the Sectional tournament games on Muncie Central's home floor at the Muncie Field House.

The Bearcats were to use this advantage many times even into the Semi-state games until well after we were adults. This is an advantage that you never hear Bearcat fans speak of to this day. I have thought several times over the years that if we could have taken on the Bearcats on our small home floor the outcomes would have been impacted. This would have been especially true during my last two years of high school when we were defeated both years in the final game of the sectional by the Bearcats on their home floor.

Prep Cage Ratings

As a testament to this are the ratings of none other than Dr. E.E. Litkenhous' Prep Cage Ratings for the State of Indiana. Covering all schools before schools were allocated to divisions based on enrollment, the system was strictly quantitative based on scores of previous games. There was no home court offset nor was there any consideration for the quality of an opponent. Above all, there was no politicking by the larger metro areas. It was not a popularity contest voted on by the Indiana sports writers.

What I am saying is that during the 1957-1958 season, Harrison Township found itself in some mighty fine company including eventual state champ Fort Wayne Southside. The Cardinals were first ranked 13th, then 16th, 12th, 12th and finally 11th in the last ranking issued. Keep in mind, again, this was all schools regardless of size. That last rating list looked like this:

1. Fort Wayne Southside, the eventual state champion
2. Fort Wayne Central
3. Huntingburg
4. Indianapolis Technical
5. Jeffersonville
6. Terre Haute Garfield
7. Kokomo
8. Vincennes
9. South Bend Central
10. Shawswick
11. **Harrison Township**
12. Indianapolis Shortridge
13. Calumet Township
14. Indianapolis Crispus Attucks
15. Fort Branch
16. Michigan City
17. South Bend Saint Joseph
18. Anderson
19. Springs Valley

20. Fort Wayne Concordia
21. Evansville Bosse
22. Lafayette Jefferson
23. Indianapolis Ben Davis
24. Elwood
25. Muncie Central

With a home court advantage, or at least a neutral court and Coach Boggs, what should it have been? Our case is rested.

"I'm getting ahead of myself, Gib, so let me get back to the Boggs Brothers."

But one thing that still bothers me, I digress again because of its import, is that after a very successful basketball year as a Junior, and two baseball championships as sophomore and the summer of my Junior year, Bob left us and went to his alma mater, Selma High School as I just mentioned. Coach might have left a year later perhaps, but not that year when we were primed to reach new heights during the basketball season. The only time that I ever recall feeling empathy for an opponent was when we played Selma during my last year and had our way with the overmatched and shorter Bluebirds directed by Coach Boggs. We ended up on top by a score of 76 to 21 and barely played the first half. That just didn't seem very fair to Coach Boggs who had coached us during our development years.

Bob was a year older than Phil. Selma would win the County Basketball Tournament when Bob was a Junior, when he was a Senior and Phil was a Junior and then after Bob graduated and Phil was a senior. So, they were champs in 1944, 1945 and again in 1946. As high school boys of this age and time, I am sure that World War II played heavily on their minds as they proceeded toward graduation.

The Boggs story would not be complete without recognizing all in the amazing family of Plummer and Hilda Boggs. They are the parents of five children; Keith the first born in 1920, Louise born in 1922, Edwin born in 1924, Coach Bob, and Phil a year younger than Bob.

Raising a brood of five in the depression years was challenging economically. The Boggs family was extremely self sufficient and hard working. Plummer Boggs used to keep fifty to fifty-five milk cows from 1930 forward. Do you know how many that is, especially when they had to be milked twice a day? All the cows were milked by hand until 1938 when a Surge milking machine was purchased and used while another cow was milked by hand. That's still seventeen to eighteen cows to be milked by hand. I now know from which that iron clad hand shake came.

Plummer also farmed four hundred acres and kept horses, mules, sows and pigs. You just had to feed those kids someway. Normally, the boys had to be in the barn in the mornings by 4 AM and have the horses, hogs and cattle fed and milked by 7 AM in order to catch the school bus by 7:30 AM. And you think you worked hard. During harvest season, the wagons loaded with corn would come in after dark, having been hand shucked by two hired hands. The evening meal was served around seven thirty or eight o'clock. And then, it was shoveling the loads of corn by lantern. Finishing by 11 PM was an early completion. Remember, the next day started at 4 AM. I'm fatigued just writing about this.

Once, in January 1933, the family lost all its buried potatoes and apples because of rot and rats. According to Keith, the eldest of the Boggs siblings, "You talk about a tragedy! We lived the rest of the winter on milk toast and black apple butter that you could buy for fifteen cents a quart. Dad had to butcher another hog so we would have enough to eat. He could have sold the hog for four dollars." If this doesn't rouse your sense of admiration and sensitivities then you are reading the wrong book.

Eddie Boggs

In their early athletic careers, the Boggs boys attended Royerton High School. Bob and Phil's older brother Eddie, was himself an outstanding athlete. During the 1940-1941 basketball season, Eddie was a regular on the high school varsity and Bob played for the eighth grade boys who won the county championship with Bob being selected to the all tournament team.

The next season would find the Boggs brothers playing for the Selma Bluebirds. If the boosters of the Redbirds from Royerton had known what they had lost they would have had very heavy hearts for the next several years as they had also lost Phil Boggs, the youngest of these three. Bob Barnet describes it this way as he introduced the Bluebirds season in the Muncie Newspapers. Talking of Bud Graham, the Selma coach, "he picked up a mighty good man when Edwin Boggs, a regular at Royerton last year, moved into the township. Boggs is likely to be a regular and his brother Bob, a freshman is looked upon as a comer." What an understatement that was. Eddie was listed as a 5'9"Senior and Bob as a 5'8" freshman.

In the county tournament this year, Eddie would be named to the all county tournament first team and was the leading scorer of tournament. Selma was runner up to winner Gaston, losing the championship game be a mere two points. The next year, Eddie again would lead the Bluebirds to the second place trophy and would be named again to the all tournament team. Not bad for Bob and Phil to follow up and utilize the Boggs athletic genes.

The following year, 1942-1943, the Bluebirds would be tournament runners up to Royerton with Eddie, a senior, being named to the all tournament second team. So here we are, Eddie is now gone and the Bluebirds have finished second best two years in a row.

What will Selma do now? The answer is simple, they would be champions for the next three years.

Bob Boggs

In Bob's junior year, 1943-1944, Selma would beat Yorktown in the final game with Bob topping the all tournament first team along with a couple of other notables, namely Phil Hodson from Yorktown who would later lead Gaston to a couple of championship in the 1950's, and

Mel Grove from DeSoto who would be one of our outstanding math teachers at Harrison during the 1950's. Bill Langdon from Selma was named to the second team and was also a teacher at Harrison during the same period as Mel. The third team would list John Craig from DeSoto another 1950's instructor at Harrison. Boy did we get the good ones at good old HHS.

In Bob's senior year Selma would again prevail as champions. The all tournament first team would again list Bob, Mel Grove, and John Craig but also would include Phil Boggs the youngest of the Boggs brothers. In the finals, the Bluebirds defeated the Panthers of DeSoto including both Mel Grove and John Craig. So now you have it, in four years the Boggs clan had led Selma to two championships and to two runners up finishes. Not bad for a hardworking group who arose at 4 AM and sometimes retired at 11 PM .

And here's one that you absolutely must commit to memory. It is testimony to the character, drive and lack of quit in Coach Boggs' makeup. Following the tournament, the local press described it this way, "In the final game it was the fine leadership and scoring power demonstrated by Bob Boggs, Selma veteran that paced the Bluebirds to victory. Bob found time to register 17 points", *only four points short of the opposing DeSoto Panthers, and half of Selma's total,* "while directing the team's offensive and defensive operations.

After the final game it was discovered he had been playing with a broken hand. X-ray examinations revealed the injury but the stouthearted player did not reveal his condition until after the battle. He was closely followed by brother, Phil, in scoring and ably aided by big Doug Chalfant in garnering rebounds.". This says it all about Coach Boggs, outstanding athlete, somewhat quiet in demeanor, good to the final gun, and one of the most selfless and self-effacing people that I have ever known.

The Bluebirds were to learn just how important Bob was to their line up, as they went on to lose some games while Bob was mending and lose out on the seasonal record percentage race. In the local Sectional tournament they would lose to Muncie Central by a mere four points with the Bearcats netting a tip-in at the buzzer.

Coach Boggs, just graduated, would go into the military service on the day that Germany surrendered and the European Theater was secured. It seemed as though a higher power was with him, much like when he would do the impossible in high school athletics, as the first atomic bomb was to hit Hiroshima on the day Coach graduated from basic training. He would spend a year with the occupation troops in Japan but would not be faced with being involved in the despicable carnage of battle prior to our prevailing in this, our last world war.

While in Japan, Bob would continue his athletic exploits, playing baseball in the American League of Japan for the Eighth Army Chicks and some football in the American Football League of Japan for the same Eighth Army Chicks. The baseball team would win the league the season that Bob was there, tearing up opponents with a long winning streak.

It is noteworthy, that several professional level fellows played with him. Perhaps just as noteworthy, is that the coach of the Ball State Cardinal football team approached Bob, after his military service stint, and inquired if he would like to play football for Ball State. Bob, being his usual bright but diplomatic self, declined but related to me recently that "he didn't want to be the tackling dummy for the more experienced players". Coach and high school teammate, Don Schumaker, would later try out with the Pittsburgh Pirates organization as the Pirates barnstormed through the Muncie area. Coach as an outfielder-pitcher, Schumaker as an outfielder.

After receiving his initial degree from Ball State in 1950, Coach would go on to his illustrative coaching-teaching career. Coach was to earn his graduate degree from BSU later. Coach was to retire in 1989, having coached and taught for 39 years. He had won six county baseball championships, one sectional and one regional game. Starting the golf program at Wapahani in 1968, he won the first county golf league championship. Coach would again step up when he started the first basketball program for girls at Wapahani when his daughter was a freshman. When his daughter was a senior, they would win the first

ISHAA tourney held at Randolph Southern. His girls' teams would win two county championships and two sectionals.

In 1986, Coach was elected to the Delaware County Athletic Hall of Fame. There should not be a single detractor for this well earned recognition. Coach lists playing with his brother Phil as his most memorable experience as an athlete and starting the girls basketball program and golf program at Wapahani as his best remembered achievements as a coach. And incidentally, Coach didn't just teach the game of golf and how to avoid a slice, he netted a hole-in-one at the Cardinal Hills Golf Course in 1995. Coach still couldn't get away from us Cardinals.

Coach and his brother Phil were not above the detractions of adolescence, however, as they were both suspended for skipping school as high school students.

Phil Boggs

Playing on three consecutive county championship teams at Selma, Phil Boggs would lead the 1946 Bluebirds to a season record of 19-5. This was the first year following Bob's graduation and entry into service in the military. Phil led all scorers in the county, scoring 300 points. Let me tell you, that's quite a few for that time when scores seldom surpassed forty-five or fifty.

Phil had some physical dominance as a senior, coming in at 6'3 ½" and weighing in at over 180 pounds. Following the sectional, local sports writers would say, "It also appears the three-year reign of the Selma Bluebirds as county champions is not likely to continue. Earl Snider loses Phil Boggs, **rated by many as the best player in the sectional".** So there you have it---Phil not only was good, he was the best of the best. Phil was named to the all sectional first team this year.

At the beginning of the 1945-1946 basketball season, **Coach Earl Snider** started to become recognized as the wizard he was and would be for many years to come. The Bluebird coach had put together 61 wins in his three seasons at Selma, as they had won two county tournament championships, and two seasonal percentage championships. Then in 1946, with Phil leading the way, the Bluebirds would win both the seasonal percentage championship and the county tournament. So, go figure. What a record. I recall what some would consider a small item as a senior guard for Harrison Cardinals and Coach Snider was then the mentor of the Yorktown Tigers having won more championships there with Modie Beeman and friends. We always came out on our small gymnasium floor and took the far basket away from our bench. Well this time, Coach Snider must have been looking for anything to throw us off our game since we were a tall and dominating team and his Tigers were clearly the underdogs. Knowing the rules, and being a cunning and smart leader, Coach Snider opted to have us switch baskets for the first half after having warmed up at the other basket. He clearly had that option under the rules used by the IHSAA. The good news is that it didn't work for him and we came away with a twenty-five point victory 85-60.

Our normal positions were altered for the opening tip off and I lined up on the side of the circle away from the big guys, Bill Long and John Ramsey rather than taking the defensive position at the top of Yorktown's foul circle. I whispered to Moose Ramsey just prior to the jump that I would be breaking down the side line. Moose just tipped the ball in my direction and after a couple of stutter steps and even a change of pace or two, I was able to drop an eight foot jumper cleanly in the hole. Well, the trick didn't work but I remember Earl Snider very well because of this incident.

During the 1946 county tournament, Phil Boggs led all scorers and was named to the first team all tournament team. Again the local newspaper said "Phil Boggs, the tall Selma center, led the scoring for the tournament with 14 fielders and 10 fouls for 38 points. Boggs was in four games, but played only about half of the final contest."

As an eighth grader, Phil would lead the Bluebirds to the county eighth grade championship as Brother Bob had done one year earlier at Royerton. I remember Coach Boggs inviting me and Bob Murphy to travel to the Fort Wayne Semi-State Tournament with him and Phil in 1954. That was my first meeting with Phil. We had a wonderful time traveling up in Coach's sparkling new Pontiac Chiefton and seeing Muncie Central's Bearcats play. The irony, if there was one, is that this was the year that we also won the City-County YMCA eighth grade tourney as both Boggs brothers had done earlier. It was also the year of the Milan Indians and Bobby Plump and company.

In January, 1971, Phil was recognized for his athletic achievements when he was named to a twelve member Lions 25-D Silver Anniversary Basketball Team. Denver Wooten for Muncie Central was also named as was "jumping" Johnny Wilson from state champion Anderson.

Phil was also elected into to the Delaware County Athletic Hall of Fame in 1987 a year after Coach's induction. That's quite a feat some 40 years after finishing competition.

Phil says his most memorable achievement was playing with his older brother Bob. Now that's brotherly love.

The Reunion, November 24, 2006

L to R: Standing, John Wray, Bob Boggs, Ralph Wray
Front: Phil Boggs

Selma Bluebirds 1944
County Champions

Front Row L to R: Bob Boggs, Bill Langdon, Kenneth Main, Bobby Pittenger, Ron Madill. Second Row L to R: Coach Earl Snider, Don Schumaker, Dick Coon, Doug Chalfant, Sam Williams, Gene Sheward, Jim Owens, Mgr.
Front: Mascot Bobby Gimore

Photograph furnished courtesy of the Star Press

Selma Bluebirds 1945
County Champions

Front Row L to R: John Smidley, Charles Scott, Luther Wells, Mgr., Don Schumaker, Jack Paul.
Secon Row L to R: Coach Earl Snider, Gene Sherwood, Phil Boggs, Doug Chalfant, Bob Boggs, Inserts: Dale Madill. Dick Coon

Selma Bluebirds 1946
County Champions

Front Row L to R: Bob Ruble, Jack Paul, Lowell Goodwin, Charles Scott, Dick Hiatt. Second Row L to R: John Smidley, Merril Engle, Coach Earl Snider, Phil Boggs, Jim Engle, Herb Main

Photographs furnished courtesy of the Star Press

Plummer Boggs' Sons 1942
Front Edwin and Bob Boggs,
Back Keith and Philip Boggs

Edwin Bogg, 1941

Coach Earl Snider, 1940's
Photograph furnished courtesy of the Star Press

Bob Boggs, 1944-45

Bob Boggs receives Trophy, 1945

Selma Bluebirds receive their trophy, 1945,
Phil Boggs on far left, Bob Boggs on far right

Phil Boggs, 1946

Photographs furnished courtesy of the Star Press

8th Army Chicks, Japan
W29 L13
1946

Bob Boggs, first row left

(L) Coach Boggs, (R) Pitcher Leon Gore
Japan 1946

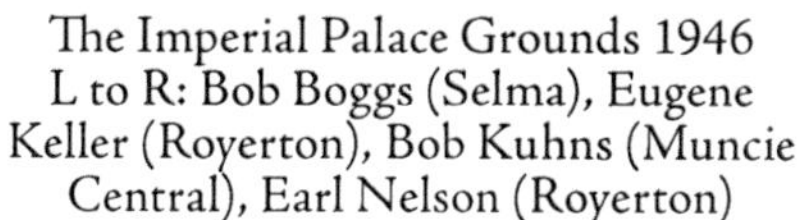

The Imperial Palace Grounds 1946
L to R: Bob Boggs (Selma), Eugene Keller (Royerton), Bob Kuhns (Muncie Central), Earl Nelson (Royerton)

Lions ClubDistrict 25-D
Silver Anniversary Team, January 28, 1971

Phil Boggs back row on left
Photograph furnished courtesy of the Star Press

Coach Boggs
Delaware County Hall of Fame 1985

Coach Boggs,
Hole in One - 1995

Chapter Seven

Taylor Hayes

One of the least talked about coaches and leaders, from Delaware County was Taylor Hayes, who led the Eaton Norsemen from 1947 to 1952, and then coached the Albany Wildcats from 1952 to 1956. From the Wildcats, Taylor would go to Sweetser High School in Indiana. He always produced winners every where he landed. He would cap his career at William Penn College, in SE Iowa where he now resides in the College's Hall of Fame.

The Eaton players that stand out in Taylor's mind are none other than Jim Taylor and Jack Tapy. He says what he also needed to support these guys was a good point guard, but no one was smart enough.

At Albany, Ted Fullhart, who would later play at Ball State University, a 6-4 forward by the name of Smith who was an exceptional outside shooter, Errol Washburn and Rex St. John stood out as guards.

Taylor left for Sweetser where he remained from 1956 to 1959. While there, the record was 47 wins and 12 losses. Sweetser was beaten in the state tournament by number one ranked Marion. While there he was contacted by three colleges that had head coach openings.

He ended up at William Penn where they had had eighteen straight losing seasons. In fact, five of those seasons were without a single win. Taylor's record turned out to 208 wins and only 35 losses. Taylor had recruited three of the Marion stars, and in total, twelve boys from Indiana.

He recalls a game against number 20 nationally ranked Murray State (Kentucky) when they fell by 4 or 5 points. Sounds like the Cardinals and Muncie Central doesn't it.

Taylor Hayes received a standing ovation when he returned to William Penn for his induction into their Hall of Fame. Nothing else need be said about this great one who now lives in the Muncie area.

Chapter Eight

The Bearcats and Their Traditions

High school basketball in Indiana is unlike any other high school sport played anywhere in the USA. It stands alone as the center of social activities in large and small communities. It has produced numerous books and many outstanding athletes. And, Muncie Central stands head and shoulders above all others in terms of their success.

For instance, Muncie Central leads the pack in having won eight state championships. But it doesn't end there. They also lead the pack in having played in the final championship game thirteen times, been in the final four seventeen times, been in the final eight twenty-five times and the final sixteen thirty-one times. Need I say more?

There are a number of reasons for this in my view. They have a very strong tradition and have feeder schools for Junior High Schools that are many times larger in themselves than most of the other schools in Delaware County. As an eighth grader, playing on an undefeated team from Harrison Township, with maybe 40 boys in the seventh and eighth grades, we were able to defeat Wilson, Blaine and McKinley along with the largest in the county, Royerton. Then in high school, after all the feeder schools amassed at Muncie Central, we were twice outgunned by the Bearcats in the finals of the Sectional tournament in my Junior and Senior years.

It was a mountain to be climbed as we had no feeder system, played a much easier schedule, played in a small gymnasium, and faced the Bearcats on their home floor where they not only played their home games but also practiced all season long. This is not sour grapes since the Bearcats deserve the reputation they have earned over the years. I also think that we were under achievers since our youth and immaturity got in our way.

Dick and Jackie Stodghill, in their excellent history of Bearcat basketball list the records of the Bearcats versus other schools they have played over the years. In reviewing this data I am astounded. Of the other schools in Delaware, excluding Muncie Burris, through 1988, the Bearcats won 172 of 182 contests. This is a 94.5% winning percentage. If you exclude Yorktown, who defeated the Bearcats five times, the percentage rises to 96.7%. In the years 1954 through 1958, my high school years, the Bearcats were in the Final Four twice, the Final Eight three times, and the final Sixteen five times. It was an uphill battle for us with slightly more than 100 high school students counting both sexes.

But let's give them credit. Muncie Central has produced many outstanding athletes, college and professional. At the risk of overlooking someone here are the ones that I remember from the 1950's and early 1960's. Tom Harold, Charlie Mock, Jim Hinds, Gene Flowers, Jerry Lounsberry, Charlie Hodson, Danny Thornburg, Ron Bonham, Mike Rolf, John Isenbarger, Bill Dinwiddie, Jim Davis, John Dampier, Rick Jones, Glender Torain and Andie Higgins. How would you like to have them in your line up?

Then there were Art Beckner and Jay McCreary, both players and coaches of state champion Bearcats. You can't argue with the talent but then you wonder if you could have gotten them on your home court. The small size alone would have had an impact.

Well maybe!

As I said earlier, you can't help but admire this tradition. They are, in some respects, like the Greek hero Hercules.

1956-57 Graduating Bearcats

Ted Sterrett **Dean Campbell** **Bill O'Neal**

Henry Johnson **George Burks** **Dave Satterfield**

Photographs furnished courtesy of the Star Press

Chapter Nine

The Pre-School Years—Some Anecdotes

"Gib", I said, "want to hear about how Johnny Hoosier developed?"

Gib asked me to talk about anything I could recall during my preschool days. I thought and thought and finally said, 'I think I can relate a couple of experiences." One dealt with my first lesson in family values and the love between my parents and their concern for me and my siblings.

This was during the height of WWII and about the time that the Allies under General Dwight Eisenhower were planning their invasion at Normandy in an attempt to drive the Nazis out of France and to commence the retaking of mainland Europe. I would later learn that it was the costliest effort in terms of casualties and equipment in the entire history of the despicable thing we call war. At any rate, I noticed that my Mother became very hesitant to walk out to our mailbox, which was only about a 100 yards from our house on Godman Avenue in West Muncie, regardless of the weather. I was 4 or 5 years old at this time. It reached the point where Mom asked me to go out each day to retrieve our mail. Finally she said to all us kids that she was deeply afraid that my Father was going to be drafted by the military even with a 3A classification (because of his three sons). She was very much afraid not only for my Dad but also for our welfare and how she would provide for herself and us kids. We were a struggling young family and money was not in overabundance. I finally agreed that I would fetch the mail daily and bring it to her. I had thought to myself that if I found anything looking official from the government that I would simply dispose of it and not tell her. Little did I know, at the time, that my father might be incarcerated for failing to report for induction. Fortunately, no notice came from the military, and after Japan's surrender, the war was over. This was my earliest remembrance of family love for each other and in particular, the love my parents had for each other.

Lesson Learned: Family Love Can be Very Strong

Another experience while we lived on Godman Avenue involved our friends next door, Bobby and David Miller. We had gotten to know them quite well as any group of young boys would. David was the same age as my older brother John who was two years older than I. Bobby was just a year younger and a year older than I.

The four of us were all over the area surrounding our homes and had found just the right place for our "hideout". A small barn quite removed from our house but only a couple of hundred yards back. It had a perfect loft area where we had set up our play-living area. One day one of us had the bright idea that we should all pack a lunch and celebrate our good fortune and eat in the loft.

I remember having sandwiches and vegetables and bringing milk as our drink. John and I didn't bring enough milk for refills and I soon found out that my glass was empty. Needles to say, both David and Bobby took notice of my predicament and gave me another glass from their ample supply. I gladly took it but can't even remember if I had the social skills to say thank you. We had a glorious celebration at the opportunity to play adults. Of course, brother John promptly reported the incident to our Mother who quickly told me, in no uncertain words, that I should not have accepted this minor hand out from David and Bobby. We didn't accept handouts from anyone. We earned it ourselves or we did without. We were close friends with David and Bobby even after they moved out on Wheeling Avenue north of town.

Lesson Learned: Earn Your Keep and be Hesitant in Accepting Things You Haven't Earned

"Gib", I said, "if you're not too bored, I can relate two other stories that occurred maybe a year of two prior to this." Gib, of course, was all ears.

The initial one deals with my first experience with the protective instincts of mothers even though this involves birds—Blue Jays that is. John, my mother and I, were out in our vegetable garden. While I don't remember why we were there, what I do remember is that I suddenly came upon some baby Blue Jays that had not reached the stage where they had found the freedom of flight. Being an inquisitive type even at that age, I proceeded to follow the small and delicate off springs and picked up the first one that I could coral. Suddenly, without any pre-warning, the mother Blue Jay landed on my towhead and proceeded to peck my head incessantly. Quickly I released the baby Blue Jay and left the vegetable garden. Later I would muse that even birds are extremely protective of their young.

Lesson Learned: A Mother's Protective Instinct is Very Strong

Another recollection is a little more painful than the pecks from the mother Blue Jay. I recall that my Grandmother (Baldock) Wray was visiting and we were all having breakfast around our kitchen table. Across the room, and a step lower was our living room. We had a pot bellied stove in the living room for heating our house.

For some reason the front door to our living room was ajar, slightly open. My parents asked John if he would go close the front door. I don't recall why John didn't do it, but do recall that my parents then turned to me and asked if I would do it. I promptly complied but as I turned to return to the kitchen, I fell. Right into the hot pot bellied stove. I think they called them Warm Morning Heaters back then.

Well this one was not only warm, it was hot. Extremely hot. What I recall is that I had not previously felt so much pain. It was pain that just couldn't be reduced or alleviated. While my Grandmother held me in my bedroom and said all the comforting things she could most of that day I thought the pain would never go away.

The good news is that the burns were minor and soon dissipated. The remembrance is that I realized that there was something called pain, intense pain.

Lesson Learned: Physical Pain Can be Overwhelming

Mom (r), Aunt Fonzie (l) as teenagers

Dad in his courting days

"Gib", I said, "another thought occurred to me which concerns a life long friend, who at 5 years old, learned about honesty and respecting the property of others." Gib wanted to hear this and gave me his standard hand signal to get it on. I waited as Gib ordered up another batch of his favorite catfish. "Gib", I said, "my friend Phil Glaze went with his mother to a grocery in Gaston, Indiana, as a 5 year old." While there, he picked up a hickory nut unnoticed by the store owner or his mother. Upon arrival home, Phil showed his mother the contents of his pocket. Horrified, his mother promptly put Phil back in their car and took him back to the grocery and told Phil to tell the owner about his hickory nut. As Phil relates now, he learned this lesson early and very well. Phil, an outstanding athlete in high school, is now a member of the Delaware County Athletic Hall of Fame for his post high school exploits in softball.

Lesson Learned: Honesty First

Chapter Ten

Elementary School Years--Some Anecdotes

"Gib, let me now relate some of the things that occurred during my elementary years." Gib, being the gentleman that he is, was again, all ears.

My older brother John and I had an interest in sports at an early age. I'm not sure how this developed since our Dad had never encouraged us much since he was always very busy earning our keep. Most time he worked two jobs. As the oldest surviving son of a family of six siblings, he had been forced to stop his education after his eighth grade year when my grandfather was unexpectedly killed in a traffic accident. From that point forward, Dad was the patriarch of the family and was expected to continue eking out a living on the family farm.

He did this until he had a family of his own and three small sons, John, myself and my younger brother Donald 'Rudy'. Later on, after relocating to Delaware County, Indiana, our youngest brother Jim came along some eleven years my junior.

I recall clearly the day Jim was born. It was a hot summer day, high in humidity. I had been out on my bicycle at a friend's house and returned home shortly after noon.

I don't recall how we had gotten the word from Ball Memorial Hospital but clearly recall that my brothers and I mused that it wasn't a girl which my parents had been talking about all during the pregnancy. They wanted a girl to go with their houseful of boys. It is probably just as well since one girl, the youngest of the siblings, would have been spoiled beyond reason. Jim would go on to letter two years for the Muncie Central Bearcats in basketball. If only he would have had some of my tenacity and I would have some of his height, we both could have been better.

Later on it was my Aunt Marjorie who reminded all of us just how responsible John was, even at age 13, because he dutifully called to tell her of Jim's birth while Dad was still at the hospital. This is a trait that John demonstrates to this day. He always made me look bad in this regard. Aunt Marge is the mother of our cousin, Bernie Smith, who unfortunately passed at age 49, but was a four year starting lineman for Royerton's football teams, graduating in 1959. A couple, or more, of those Redbird teams were undefeated.

Lesson Learned: Be Responsible

Royeron Redbird Football Team
October 10, 1956

Cousin Bernie Smith #30

I digress. "Gib" I said, "let me get back to my original thoughts." Gib mused, "I wish you would."

Even though John and I independently developed our interest in sports we did have some support for Dad even with his work schedule. The story line is that we had just returned home from town with our first baseball gloves and a brand new hardball. Baseballs were called hardballs back then; I suppose to differentiate them from softballs. At any rate, if wasn't five minutes into our pitch and catch game that I wound up and fired the ball way above John's head straight into our bedroom window. No one had yet mentioned that I should set my feet first before letting it rip. Actually, with all my errant throws later on, maybe no one ever said that to me. Or at least, I never got the message. The errant overthrow hit the window with a thunderous clash and sailed all the way into our bedroom.

At age seven, I had attained the first of, what would turn out to be many errant overthrows. I always seemed to focus on velocity rather than accuracy. Most of the time it worked out but other times it was disastrous. Afterwards, after we retrieved our brand new baseball, John and I switched places so I would be throwing towards our vegetable garden and he, with his better accuracy, would throw in the direction of our house.

Lesson Learned: Get to Know Skill Level First

"Gib", I said, "this next one is one is actually pre-school but I just thought of it and don't want you to miss it. I don't fully comprehend even to this day." When I was five years old and Dad was doing some things for Mr. Walter Fisher on his farm, I asked Dad if I could back the small Allis-Chalmers tractor out of the storage building. We were to trail a wagon through the freshly harvested corn fields to salvage as much of the corn that the corn picker had missed. Actually, as high school students in the 50's, our classmates and I would do this in the various fields around our school and sell the corn to raise money for our senior trip to Washington, DC. We were frugal out of necessity in those days.

After Dad gave his OK, I remember jumping up in the seat and then to my consternation realizing that not only did I have to start this thing but I also had to put the thing in reverse. I had to guess where reverse was. I was lucky and got it right and we backed out without incident. A forward gear would surely have sent us right through the back side of the implement shed. Fortunately it was a small tractor so it all worked out. I am sure that Dad never recanted this to Mom.

The hardest part was to drive that thing a few yards forward and stop while Dad and a helper picked up the corn and put it in the corn wagon that we pulled behind the tractor. You see, I would push the clutch in and hold it in every time we stopped rather than mess with the gears since I had no knowledge of the gear pattern. My five year old leg would kill me every time we stopped. It seemed like an eternity before they would tell me to move on and I could release the clutch.

Lesson Learned: Waiting to Do Some Things is Being Smart

"Want to go back to the elementary years"? I asked Gib. Sure enough he did.

When I started my formal schooling, John was in the third grade. This was at Cowan School which was located in southern Delaware County. This was a K-12 school with no kindergarten in those days. My first day started with some difficulty. There was a girl sitting close to me that was crying unabashedly. Soon, two or three boys started to get caught up in the same fervor of the moment---crying. While the teacher, Mrs. Reynolds, a smartly dressed and beautiful young woman, tried to console those that were crying. Sure enough, I soon found that my eyes were getting wet but couldn't understand why. It took me a minute or so to get control of myself. That was the end of it and everything was great thereafter.

Lesson Learned: Growth is Good but Can be Stressful

In another incident that occurred about this time, John, I and an older friend about John's age, were out in the countryside on our bikes. It may have been Norm Barton, a neighbor, who would later star for the Cowan Blackhawk basketball teams. After riding a couple of hours, we stopped at a bridge on some gravel country road. Most were still gravel in those days so this is of little help in recalling just where we were. We wanted to take a look at the shallow water in the creek bed to see if per chance some fishing might be possible since there were few, if any, places to fish in this flat agricultural farming area.

As we sat on the edge of the top of this bridge, we saw several electrical lines that were close to us as they were strung across this creek bed. After a few minutes, Norm asked if I would like to touch one of the wires in front of us and within easy reach. He said if you get a stick and reach out you will be able to touch one of the wires with some ease. Better yet, if you get a fresh stick, and peeled off the outside bark, it would be easier. Norm indicated that you wanted a fresh, clean and wet stick.

After some major daring; my instincts took over as I was not one to back away from a dare even in those days. I found the stick, peeled it back and had my wet and clean stick ready for action. I touched the line which fortunately was probably low in voltage, and got the biggest shock of my young life. What a jolt it was and I tended to evaluate dares a little more thoroughly after that.

Lesson Learned: Think for Yourself and Be Aware of Personal Risk

When I reached the third grade, we relocated to a small home with minor acreage on Bethel Pike which was Northwest of Muncie. It was to be the first home purchased by my parents following their migration from Kentucky and the family farm of my grandparents. John and I transferred to Harrison Township School, another K-12 school in Western Delaware County. Again, there were twelve grades under one roof with no kindergarten.

My first day was pretty uneventful, since our teacher, Mrs. Florence Gwaltney, had not had an opportunity to introduce me to my classmates and to provide for my social welfare. Then it was time for the morning recess. This was an interesting class since we had about 40 third graders and 8 or 10 fourth graders that had been transferred in from Center Township. In those days the elementary grades, which were the first grade through the sixth grade, had a 30 minute morning recess, a lunch break and an afternoon 30 minute recess.

No Xbox or Play Station for us, we got a lot of exercise during these periods and would never become couch potatoes. As we prepared to break for the morning recess, on this my first day at Harrison, the boy in front of me asked if I would like to play with him during the break. Of course I said yes, since I didn't know anyone in the class as yet.

His name was Herbie Jones and I didn't find out until later that he came from a challenged background. Herbie was bused in for Center Township and as a small slightly built third grader was, as I found out later, ostracized by our other classmates. He had no one else with which to play. In getting to know the social structure later on I came to realize that Herbie came from deprived circumstances. He struggled greatly with his studies, was economically deprived and even in need of some hygiene counseling. Over the years I have thought of Herbie a few times and wondered what ever happened to him since he did not finish high school with us. I still like Herbie a lot although we rarely spent time together after that first recess at Harrison and our trying to swing higher than anyone else that day.

If I had only known then, what I have come to realize over the years, maybe I could have helped him.

Lesson Learned: Be Aware of the Underdog and Have Compassion for All Humankind

"Gib", I said, "since there are so many outstanding musicians here around Dale Hollow and between here and Nashville, would you like to hear about my aborted attempt at becoming a virtuoso?" My man Gib was ready.

When John and I were in the fourth and sixth grades, or somewhere close to that time, we were told by our parents that we were going to take music lessons. Our instructor was to be a distinguished man in Muncie, Mr. Ward Ellison, a very accomplished violinist. He would treat his students by playing for us at the end of our weekly lessons. He was great on that violin---or is it fiddle?

We were told by Mom and Dad that we could take lessons on the violin or the steel guitar. John had decided that his forte would be the violin and I, although I favored the steel guitar even back then, agreed I would also try the violin since John and I could go together every week for our lessons and Mom and Dad would only have to travel into town once rather than going a separate and second time for lessons. Maybe my heart wasn't in it which could have been the reason for my flexibility.

We were apparently doing quite well as we started because we were asked to join a select group of Mr. Ellison's best students for an additional lesson every week which would be free instruction. I thought that was validation of my budding talents but soon found that John was the only one of us that consistently spent an hour of practice each day. I, of course, started to fall behind in my skill development which led to a rising dislike for the musician's world. I seemed to have too many other things I wanted to do rather than practice.

Eddie Miller, a few years John's senior, and who was first violist in our high school orchestra back then, volunteered to give us lessons during the school day. Eddie would come to my homeroom and fetch me for a lesson. While I didn't mind being excused from class, I soon forgot to bring my violin to school on the days we were to practice with Eddie. Eddie finally stopped coming around to fetch me for my lesson. He knew the level of my interest had wavered. If I would have chosen later on, I would have picked the steel guitar and may have been playing today in some country western group. Maybe.

Our interest in music today is broad and varied because we are very much in awe of such greats as Andrew Lloyd Webber, Michael Crawford's powerful voice, Mandy Patinkin and his perfect tenor voice, James

Galway and his famous flute, Beethoven's Symphony No. 5, Alabama, George Strait, Vince Gill, Carrie Underwood and many others.

Lesson Learned: If It Is Worth While It Takes Hard Work

"Gib, let me tell you about our introduction to modern plumbing. This was about the same time as my aborted violinist career." Gib was ready again.

My dad decided, with a lot of encouragement I am sure from my mother, that modern plumbing was a must. While this was desperately needed, John and I would find out with some discomfort that we were going to save some of the cost of construction and installation by digging the drainage line ditches and the huge hole for the systems septic tank. It was huge, or at least it seemed to a young lad.

The digging of the drainage ditch line went rather quickly but then we were ready for the septic tank hole. With picks and shovels we toiled away for a number of days, wanted to curse every time we tried to loosen more of that hard, rock like clay that was down six, seven or eight feet below the surface. We didn't know how to curse. Besides our parents would have disowned us if they ever heard us utter a profanity, so we figured out every reason we could conjure up as to how we had other things that we simply had to do.

As least I did. I even used home work to get out of digging. That was the only time in my educational history, other than much later in college, when I did any of my home work assignments. John was by all accounts just the opposite since he later was awarded a Storer Scholarship and a full ride for his undergraduate years. Not me.

Finally, when we were finished, thanks to Dad's efforts, the construction process was completed. A single sink, toilet and a standard sized bathtub with a shower above it, was our first introduction to modern plumbing. Quite different from the amenities that we enjoy today. However, we were not as modern as you could be since our first television was to come a few years later.

Lesson Learned: Things That Are Worthwhile Require Effort

"Gib, these elementary years would not be complete without a couple of athletic stories since the real focus of my story to you will be athletics as we grew older." Gib wanted to hear this immediately.

One of my early introductions to athletics occurred in the fourth grade class of Mrs. Bernice Oliver. At Harrison Township we had regular basketball games during our lunch break in the high school gym. One year we were even coached by members of the varsity team. Our coach was none other than Larry Campbell, a star athlete in baseball and basketball who would later go on to start for Ball State's varsity basketball team and an outstanding administrator for Indiana University. Larry was a role model back then when we didn't even know what a role model was.

After stuffing down our food, in about two minutes, we were ready to take on all comers in a short game of basketball, complete with high school boys as officials. Most of the scores were very low since the games were short out of necessity and our skills were not developed at that time. At least our shooting abilities had not yet showed up. It was rare that any team ever scored more than ten points during these encounters. Well, on this day I used all of my strength to get the ball just barely over the rim from the left side and the ball gently rolled through the net. We had won 2-0. What a defensive struggle it had been or was it a scoring outburst.

When we returned to the classroom Mrs. Oliver was determined to embarrass me at my tender age, and did so be raving over that single basket. It felt good to be recognized that way although I needed to learn how to handle it without being red faced. Later on I mused that Mrs. Oliver was a master at motivating us and developing our egos.

Lesson Learned: Work on Your Strengths and Learn to Handle Recognition with Humility

"Gib, this next one will be better. I promise." Since Gib, the master and polite gentleman that he is, would never tell me he was bored.

The first time we would experience the thrill of playing in a basketball tournament was in the sixth grade. We would travel to Gaston for a four team tournament involving Gaston, Summitville, and a third school that I can't recall, and us, the sixth graders of Harrison Township.

We were confident that we would prevail since we had three sixth graders who were actually playing regularly on our seventh grade team and its regular schedule. Bruce Carpenter, a diminutive and quick left handed guard, Tom Robbins another guard and master shooter and me, a forward, were all playing as regulars for Harrison's seventh grade troops.

Our first game was against Summitville, a school outside Delaware County, whom we knew little about. Boy what a surprise. They were good and were led by a young lad named Bruce Yeagy. Bruce was a cagey and fast little guard who would go on to star for Summitville on some of the best teams they ever put on the floor. Summitville scored first and we quickly in bounded the ball and I drove the length of the floor to score a tying lay up. I can't recall any details beyond that except I recall that we played catch up the entire game and ended up losing a close game. What an awakening that was.

Charlie Marcus, our high school coach at the time, called a time out near the end of the contest and, pointing to the tournament trophy setting on the scorers table, said, "you see that trophy on the scorers table, well if you want it you'd better get your game together." We didn't and Summitville would later claim it after winning the championship game. We won the consolation game by blowing out Gaston and doubling the score. However, we didn't get the trophy and had learned a valuable competitive lesson.

Lesson Learned: If You Think You Are Good There is Always Someone Better

"Academically" I said to Gib, "once I got to high school my performance was very much less than remarkable until I was in college and finally saw the light although I had a taste of success earlier. This is a short reiteration of one of those times." Gib suddenly seemed fascinated since he was a master scholar.

One of my first successes academically was in the fifth grade of Mrs. Elva Smith who had taught for years. A stern task master, we young folks must have been very stressful for her as she appeared to be approaching retirement. We were asked to draft an essay for a contest that would involve all of us as well as the sixth grade. I recall that we were given about two weeks to draft our masterpieces and submit them to Mrs. Smith.

The subject was loosely focused on health and hygiene. It very well could have been initiated due to the polio epidemic which was in the early stages prior to the days when we kids were under quarantine, at least for a short period, and prior to Jonas Salk's development of his vaccine for polio.

This was, of course, a major medical breakthrough and without doubt had the most impact as I grew up. I struggled with procrastination until the last day when our essays were due. Mrs. Smith nonchalantly announced that everyone that had not turned in an essay would forego their afternoon recess and work on their essay. I wasn't very pleased since I would miss our usual baseball game where we would either divide into two groups of us fifth graders or have at it when we would challenge the sixth graders who were recessed at the same time.

We did this every recess period. As I sat and tried to envision just how to draft a Pulitzer essay, I struggled and struggled. It was very difficult for me. Finally, after almost everyone else had finished and I was one of two or three students left in the classroom, I was finished. Done I thought. Is that baseball game over? It was.

The next day, to my surprise, I was announced as one of three winners in our class and had to go to the room of the more mature sixth graders for a recognition program. I was embarrassed that I had missed our baseball game and had to stand in front of all these sixth graders and recite my name. The truth is, I had a crush on one of the sixth grade girls who shall remain anonymous to her relief.

I did manage to recite my name but was red faced as one could be. This was my first public speaking experience as I recall. It took numerous group speaking experiences, later in professional life, for me to reach that magical relaxed and comfortable level. You just had to do it to be totally comfortable.

Lesson Learned: Do Not Procrastinate and Accept Recognition if you are Lucky Enough to Get it

"Gib, want to hear an interesting and family experience that occurred about a year prior to my first public speaking experience?" Of course, Gib wanted to hear.

Once, while in the fourth grade, I was at home for a week with something they called the 'pink eye'. This is an acute highly contagious conjunctivitis which affects your eyes. Although not distressed at all, I was at home because of the contagious nature of this minor affliction and had contacted it at school where it was going around. One of the school administrators had actually taken me home from school when the infection was discovered since we were a one vehicle family in those days and my mother had never bothered to get her driving license. To this day, Mom hasn't driven as she is in her 92nd year.

Unbeknownst to us, my Uncle Bob and his new bride Jody, who lived out of state since Uncle Bob was a career military man, drove up to our house. My Mother and I were the only ones at home at the time since this was in the middle of the day. After a couple of hours of adult chatter and catching up, for some reason my Mom suggested that I take my Uncle Bob and my new Aunt Jody outside and shoot some baskets where we had installed a basket on the old barn that was right behind our house. Later, I learned that my Mother wanted some space to prepare the meal we would have when my Dad returned home from work in a few minutes.

We agreed on a game of HORSE. After three quick misses I was in trouble. I recall saying to myself, "self you had better start concentrating". And I did. Although I missed another shot giving myself four misses and having HORS as my score, I did concentrate enough to sink several shots and win the game.

I recall that Uncle Bob, whom we seldom saw due to his military assignments, was very complimentary. I decided then that maybe I should try this game of basketball. Uncle Bob and Aunt Jody went on to have a full life, with children who were outstanding athletes in Louisville, Kentucky.

Lesson Learned: Know Your Strengths and Develop Them

"Gib, I'm on a roll so here's a couple more."

One story that begs for reiteration involves my older brother John and his fifth grade class taught by Mrs. Smith. This one comes from my old friend Jim Beedle, whose younger brother Dennis was a classmate of mine. Jim was John's classmate. Jim relates a time when he and his classmates, including John, were all late in returning from recess. Mrs. Smith swatted each of the boys twice but did not touch the girls. The boys, it seems were swatted once because they were late and a second time because the girls were also late. While this seems like reverse discrimination, we did not have the 1964 Civil Rights Act and later as amended in 1967. Title VII and Title IX were not part of our legal, societal and sociological spectrum.

Jim would later mention that one of his proudest moments was when he won the Delaware County Fair tractor backing contest. I wonder if he could have handled the Formula Fords at Watkins Glen, something I would do in the Skip Barber Eastern and Florida Series. While it is interesting to note that several of these budding drivers are today at the top of the open wheel racing pinnacle, we had a wonderful time in doing such tracks as Sebring, Florida, Mid-Ohio, Lime Rock Park in Connecticut and, of course, Watkins Glen in New York. Tony Kaanan,

Bryan Herta, Juan Montoya come immediately to mind. Of course they were light years beyond me in both youth and skills. If you want a high, this was the way to get it. It does have a tendency to empty your pockets at an alarming rate, however.

Lesson Learned: We are More a Balanced Society Today Than Back Then

Watkins Glen Pit Road, 1990's

Watkins Glen 1990's
Getting by an opponent coming out of the first turn.

"Gib, here's more for you."

One of the things that my older brother John and I did during our elementary years was to lay out a baseball diamond on the five acres or so that were adjacent to our home on Bethel Pike. We meticulously laid out the ninety foot bases and a sixty foot pitching board. We didn't build a pitching mound for the pitching board so the height of the pitching board never came into question.

We played and played, usually rounding up other young lads in our vicinity for hours and hours of play. It was difficult for the two of us to come up with a workable game since after the batter belted the ball over your head as a pitcher you simply had no chance of putting the batter out. The batter could round all three bases and get home before you could retrieve the ball and get to home plate for the out. However, with three players you could have an outfielder, pitcher and batter for a more interesting confrontation. The batter only had to go to first base and back to home plate before the outfielder threw to the pitcher, who would cover home plate, for the put out. We had a regular rotation in this game---batter to outfield, outfield to pitcher and pitcher to batter. We spend endless hours playing this artificial baseball game.

Today, it is hard imagine the time when we spent endless hours playing ball on this small homestead. A car wash, hotel and other major retailers anchor this shopping area. However, a stately walnut tree still stands in the middle of the car wash entrance giving validity to the time when we crushed walnuts in our back yard.

Lesson Learned: Creativity Certainly Has Its Place

"Gib, another elementary recollection involved basketball." Gib wondered if our ingenuity allowed us to layout a basketball arena. Of course not.

As a sixth grader playing for the seventh grade, we had an early home game against Eaton, also in Delaware County. The bleachers and theater chairs were packed for this game since it was an early game and the school buses hadn't left to take all the students home for the day.

I remember our coach, Charlie Marcus, calling a time out early in the game since I had committed an unheard of mistake. Eaton had a number of respectable players including Bob Simmons, a good looking and fast guard. They were somewhat of a running team even as seventh graders. I found myself isolated as the lone defensive player as Bob came rushing down to their basket.

Being naive and uninitiated as a basketball player at that time, I coolly backed up toward the basket and started looking for the number of the player I had been assigned to guard in our man-to-man defensive alignment. I must have forgotten that this was a team sport and it really didn't matter how well I covered my assignment if someone else was hitting a driving lay up. Bob scored and Charlie called the timeout and told me in no uncertain words that this was a team sport. I recall some of the older boys, and in particular Larry Hargis, sitting just behind our bench laughing uncontrollably at my mental miscue.

Lesson Learned: Teamwork and Helping Other's is Paramount

Chapter Eleven
Junior High School Years

"Gib, I want to take you through our Junior High School and High School years without checking on your interest if you don't mind. That way we can get some continuity. At least that's my goal." Gib thought that was an excellent idea and encouraged me to proceed.

With a growing interest in athletics, we used to listen to the daily broadcast of the Chicago Cubs baseball games. That was about the only time we weren't active and doing things physical. Quite unlike the youngsters of today that spend many hours each day with the Xbox or PlayStation. It was this baseball interest that led to my responding to a very small ad in the Muncie Star-Press for tryouts for the local junior baseball team that was sponsored by the local Sertoma Quarterback Club.

Now this wasn't going to be a picnic since I would have to bicycle all the way into Muncie for games and practices. At any rate my determination led me to ride into town for the appointed tryout. Our ages were 12, 13 and 14, and I was 12. At age 15 you were beyond the age limit for this league of about eight teams that were commercially sponsored by the various businesses around town.

I announced that I was a catcher but never told anyone that I had never caught in any organized game in my life. So, the manager, Garth Doyle, told me to suit up with the catcher's equipment and get behind the plate. We were at Tuhey Park, a recreational park near downtown and with a public swimming pool and tennis courts. Mr. Doyle pitched and I caught through the entire list of players including the Clements brothers, Dave Holfheinz and a fellow named Tony Toney. Dave would go on to star for the Muncie Central Bearcats in both baseball and basketball. Tony had a fascinating name and was our best hitter, both for average and with power, and was a baseball star at Muncie Central later.

The Clements brothers included a well developed third baseman, a hard throwing pitcher with a very good slider, even at his age, and an oversized catcher. Fortunately for me, the catcher was the least athletic although he led in the personality arena.

Finally it was time to play Hank Sauer, the leading homerun hitter for the Chicago Cubs at that time. I swung hard a few times and did nothing but stir up the air. Finally I connected on a hard liner to left. Finally! After that it was liners all over the outfield. I had made the team.

As a twelve year old I was excited and would do almost anything to play. I would get up every Saturday morning at 5 AM, do my stint I had with a wholesale milk delivery truck and then bicycle to our Saturday game at 1 PM. Weekday games were not as strenuous since I didn't have this schedule. As I recall the wholesale milk driver was a gentleman named Hugh Curry. Hugh was a supporter of athletics and had a nephew, Gordon Curry, who was a great star for the Burris Owls basketball team. He paid me $3 a week which was my pocket money back then.

Unfortunately, this year would come to an unexpected end for me. On Saturday, July 12, 1952, we were scheduled to play a team that included future Bearcat Phil Raisor, for the league leadership. Since the county fair was in progress not enough of our opponents could get to the game so we won by forfeit. Coach Doyle was not one to miss an opportunity for practice so he divided us into separate squads for an intra squad game. For some reason I was one of the top three batters in the top of the first inning. I don't recall whether I had a hit or a base on balls.

At any rate, I subsequently reached third base uneventfully. Then---- a passed ball and I was hell bent for home plate. Flying in at full speed, I went down into a feet first slide. Then---I caught my metal spike on the corner of a newly installed plate, which still protruded nearly an half inch above the ground, and looking down and saw my right foot at a ninety degree angle with my leg.

It was somewhat painful although I was mostly scared. I am sure that as I lay on my back and yelled it was a cacophony of discord to the other players. Mr. Doyle, ran into to home plate and picked up my ninety degree ankle and it seemed to snap more into place although it still was obviously not as it should have been.

I was taken to Ball Memorial Hospital where surgery was completed under general anesthesia. I recall sitting in a wheel chair after the recovery room waiting on Dad to come from work and pick me up. As I recall, and Dad would remember later on, I simply said as Dad approached, "we won". After all we would be the city champions even if it was by default. And that was what was important. Although more games were played that summer, we were the head of the class even though I never played baseball until the next summer when we, again, were champions.

Lesson Learned: Setbacks Will Come But Keep Doing What You Enjoy and Success Will Come

My last year with the Sertoma baseball club ended in another championship. We were pitted against Post 19, a team made up mostly of Selma boys who normally had respectable baseball teams. Post 19 had a pitcher by the name of Don Bright, a large boy for his age, a right handed pitcher with a healthy fastball but with little variety in his deliveries. Don normally succeeded by his speed and power alone. We had had a very good year and so had Post 19 who was coached by Scud East who's son Jim was a curve ball pitcher, third baseman and outfielder.

We were down 3 to 1 and we were getting into the later innings of what were seven inning games back then. Still are for that matter I guess. I was a pretty high average hitter with some power. Well, I don't know who or what interceded but I came to the plate with the bases full and we were, as I mentioned, down by two runs. This would probably be our last good chance to steal this one from Post 19 and all their overconfident players. They had a number of players who were either already playing high school ball or were poised to do so once school started in the fall. We were basically a group of sandlot type players. But we were pretty good and well coached. I can still recall Coach Doyle's "ducks on the pond". This was our bunt signal.

I had already gone down on swinging strikes twice earlier in this game which was both frustrating and, fortunately, somewhat unusual. Don came in with his usual hard one and I swung hard and only ruffled up the air. The second one came in the same way, and I only increased the air turbulence. I remember backing out of the batter's box to straighten out my head as I had now swung hard eight times and not connected. One thought—am I losing it? The third pitch was the same as the earlier ones and I swing hard again.

Whack!!!!!!! I lined a long drive to left center field between the two outfielders and couldn't help but peak at our base runners and count them off as they crossed the plate. We now led 4-3. Boy was it good to get that monkey off my back. Then, as I led off second base, I caught the shortstop, out of the corner of my eye rushing to tag me out. I dove back and was fortunate to make it safely. It was the old hidden ball trick.

No one scored from that point on and we were again champions.

Lesson Learned: When You Fail, Keep Doing What You Know You Can Do and Success Will Follow

The next year the coach of Post 19, Scud East, came by to see me at my illustrative place of employment. I had landed a job at a local drive in restaurant, the North Star. I started as their dish washer on days and the progressed to full scale soda jerk and finally to a job in their commissary where we made all the specialty ice cream and ground all their beef into sandwich patties. I did this during summers and weekends until I went to a service station as I entered my senior year in high school.

On this particular day I had garnered the choice assignment of cleaning up our trash area at the back of the property. This was well before any rules on air pollution and burning in an open pit were even in the minds of the populace and our government officials. As I stood ankle deep in trash and what not, Scud pulled up and proceeded to convince me to come over to Post 19 for the coming season. What a backdrop for a recruiting call. Since I knew a number of the players on Post 19, and they were pretty good, I agreed. Post 19 was the champion that year although I didn't get the kick out of it as I did with Sertoma since Post 19 was loaded with talent and basically couldn't do anything to avoid being champions.

Lesson Learned: Stay with Your Friends

In the seventh grade I started for the eighth grade basketball team. I recall our first game of the season at Eaton High School. I had just recovered from the broken ankle of the previous summer. At least I thought I was fully recovered. I don't even remember how the game turned out but recall vividly that near the end of the third quarter my ankle started bothering me a lot. So did I say anything? No. I must have limped around the rest of the game and probably put us Cardinals at a disadvantage. It was good that that ankle never seemed to bother me again.

Lesson Learned: Don't Keep Secrets from Your Leaders, You Are Hurting Your Teammates

I don't recall our record that year but it was very respectable. We did lose in the semi-finals of the local city-county tournament at the YMCA. Our eighth grade year was sensational and we were the undefeated city-county champions. The tournament was again at the Muncie downtown YMCA. We had defeated three major city junior high schools, Blaine, McKinley, Wilson and the largest school in the county, Royerton. Most of these city schools produced Muncie Central Bearcat players later. Don Van Dyke, Larry Wilkerson and Dave Holfheinz to name three. Holfheinz had been one of my stellar teammates on the Sertoma baseball teams.

I recall our first game that year as a true eighth grader. As I reported back into the line up sometime in the last half of the game, I looked up behind the score table as I waited to be whistled back into the game, and low and behold there stood Tony Rees with some of his fellow Eaton freshman players. Tony asked in a somewhat loud voice, "how many years have in been in the eighth grade"?

I knew immediately what had triggered this question, or was it a comment, since I had played against Tony and his classmates both in seventh and eighth grade contests even though I was only in the sixth grade and then the seventh grade. I was now in sync with my class although Tony apparently was not aware of it. I don't recall what my response was but assume Tony's question was prompted, at least in part, by the huge lead we had built over the Eaton eighth grade team. Tony would turn out to be a great high school player and was a key part of a very strong Eaton High School contingent.

Our first game in the City-County tournament that year against Blaine is of note. They were undefeated as well but we didn't know it. That was probably good. I am not sure how we pulled this one out but we trailed by a score of 30-24 and we were into the fourth quarter. Quarters were only six minutes long and we didn't score a lot. I did discover about this time that Larry Wilkerson was not as quick as I had thought and I was able to hit three driving lay ups while leaving him in the dust. Some where along the way both of us had scored another basket so we were tied at 32-32. After getting a rebound of Blaine's errant shot we headed up the floor and once again I found myself isolated against Wilkerson.

Larry lagged back so I couldn't drive around him once more. A pass came in for Bruce Carpenter and I found myself only six or eight feet from our basket on the extreme left side. I let one fly and it only hit the front of the rim. Oh no! Then, the referees whistle blew. A foul was called against Wilkerson who had fronted me on that missed shot. A timeout was called by our Coach Eli Roscoe. As we gathered around him he pointed out that only two seconds remained in the game. And, I had two opportunities to win it.

As I eyed the basket I remember thinking that free throws were not particularly my forte'. They never were. If I had mastered the art of the free toss, like brother John did, I could have increased my scoring output by at least 75%. But in this case, the good news is that the first one rimed cleanly into the basket. We were ahead and only had two more seconds left in the game. The second free throw hit the back rim and bounded off to be caught by some one that I can't even recall since the game buzzer blew before any other efforts by Blaine could be attempted. In retrospect, it was probably good to have missed the second attempt, since the opponents didn't have time to call a time out and set up a play to steal victory from us.

Although I didn't know it at the time, the score box the next day showed I had scored 20 of our 33 points. This was with the masterful support of teammates who had come to set me up very well during the course of a memorable season. You see, we had played all year without starting guard Tom Robbins who was out with rheumatic fever. Tom would come back to play with us in high school and was my guard mate in our memorable senior year.

After our on floor celebration, we headed for the dressing room. It was a very large locker room but it was shared by both teams. It was not a particular problem since it was so huge. It was located under the gym floor and as I descended into the locker room I was confronted by none other than Larry Wilkerson from Blaine's team. Larry took a swing and I was lucky to see it coming so I ducked. Larry resoundedly hit one of the metal lockers. I didn't wait to see if he had broken his hand but instead headed up to get Coach Roscoe who was still up stairs on the gym floor. Coach Roscoe came to our rescue because that was the end of it.

We were thrilled of course. Although I didn't know it at the time, we were supported by many friends in the final game including my wholesale delivery boss on Saturday, $3 as you recall after arising at 5 AM., and a very well developed eighth grader from DeSota High School, Doris Crouch. She added to my embarrassment by kissing me on the check as we celebrated our victory and undefeated season. We had gone to the movies a time or two. She was a winner although I knew little of those matters at the time. I later recall a graduate course at Ball State when she abruptly announced in our Labor Law Course that she was in the wrong course and left. She was an educator and not a business student.

The next week, we were slightly embarrassed when Coach Roscoe called all of us before an assembly of all the high school students. He even introduced each individual player, making comments on each player. As Coach Roscoe introduced me I recall him saying, "this is the player that every one expected to score all of our points. Well, in one game he only had four points so this is a team achievement". He was right. I had my first taste of foul trouble in a couple of our games and was forced to sit out a lot more than I had played. My four point game, as I recall was against Royerton. We were way behind at halftime. My first bucket came as I reentered the game late in the third quarter. One of our guys missed a free throw and I was lucky to tip it back in and the score was tied. We won this one by a couple of points.

Lesson Learned: Success is Sweet

One of the exercises that John and I used to indulge ourselves in was what became known as pitching contests. We were probably ten, eleven or twelve years old at the time. Keep in mind that I was always the wild one with velocity and John, much more controlled but with less speed.

We marked off a pitching plate and catching area that represented home plate. The backstop was the outside of the old barn at our house where the previous owners had built a chicken coop area that trailed off from the highest part of the structure, much like the porch on some homes today. It provided a very good backstop which I needed a lot. Our game was to pitch, going through the full windup, and, after we had walked an imaginary batter, we would go through the checking of runners back to the imaginary bases using the standard pitchers stretch.

The catcher would call balls and strikes with four bases on balls being a run of course. We assumed names of well know major leaguers of that era such as Robin Roberts, Don Newcomb and others. Our problem was that we did not always agree on what was a ball and what was a strike.

Of course John had less velocity but was more accurate and this game depended on accuracy. I must have been competitive and won a few times because I always liked this game very much. Maybe it was the assumption of being a major leaguer that intrigued me. I don't know.

Lesson Learned: Sportsmanship and Honesty Should Be at the Top of Your List

I only recall a couple of times in Junior High School and High School when I was involved in fisticuffs. The first couple of times it was in an organized fashion, the last couple of times were not, and, I guess you could say, were physically extemporaneous. The first time was in organized boxing contests set on the stage in our school gymnasium.

This was without headgear and mouthpieces which probably explains why we rarely had an opportunity to play Mohammed Ali. My first experience was against my friend and classmate, Bruce Carpenter. Bruce was small but very well put together and also very quick. I had watched Bruce take care of all previous opponents and then it was my turn to have a go with Bruce. I had waited and laid back in hopes that Bruce would be tired and worn down and would put up less resistance.

You see, as long as you won you would keep boxing, moving along to successive opponents. I had hoped that Bruce was ready for the tank by the time I put on the gloves. Alas, that was not the case and he gave me a red faced bashing to my embarrassment. I waited to counterpunch and was not aggressive enough and Bruce, with his shorter stature and strength, seemed to have his way with me.

A couple of years later I really put my let them punch themselves out theory to good use. I also had clearly learned that aggressiveness paid off in my first encounter with Bruce. I was very aggressive and waded right into the fray and this time I got the better of Bruce. It wasn't even close.

However, I still had an opponent, Gene Schull, waiting for me. Gene was a tall and muscular kid with a very strong punch. I moved right in and took the match to him; landing many telling blows. Gene did get in one good punch which got my attention. Fortunately, this was near the end of our encounter. I won, and thought later, that I could not remember Gene losing previously. I decided that this sport required more aggressiveness than I generally wanted to expend, and most of all, I had been lucky.

A following experience involving fisticuffs was not an organized event. The school leaders had constructed a huge outdoor basketball court on the northwest corner of the school property. It was large enough to have major basketball goals length wise on the east and west ends and two other courts which ran in the opposite directions across the shorter dimensions of the layout. On this particular day there were a number of different games going on simultaneously. Naturally, these games were going on cross wise to each other. A couple of times some older boys simply knocked our ball out of play as we were in cross traffic with their game. After they did it a third time, I was perturbed since it was obvious that they were doing it deliberately and not focusing on their game at all.

I confronted the main perpetrator, Darwin Clevenger, and quickly after a few harsh words were exchanged, I found myself in a physical altercation with Darwin. I hit him very hard right away and he went down to my surprise. He got up cursing and crying so I hit him again and he hit the cement once more. Finally, in what seemed an eternity, he was trying to get up when the bell rang signaling the end of our lunch period and telling us that we should return to the building and afternoon classes.

While I wanted to stay and finish this completely, I quickly decided that I would just return to the building and hopefully avoid some undeserved discipline. Darwin was accustomed to discipline so he was unconcerned about that and was yelling obscenities and questioning my manhood as I walked off. I never heard from the school officials and never had to use fisticuffs again as long as I was at Harrison Township School, except on my last day as a junior in high school. It was Darwin's last day as a senior so he apparently felt that he was beyond the scope of any school discipline.

My friend, Bill Long, a classmate and great basketball player and teammate, reminded me of this recently, when he and his attractive wife Helen Winningham, stopped in to visit at our lake property near Dale Hollow Lake. I had apparently let it slip from my memory. We were, again, on the outside basketball court. Darwin wanted to settle what had escaped him with me a few years earlier. Bill said I hit Darwin with a direct one to his chin and he flew backwards on his back, losing both his shoes as he sailed to his rump side. There were just too many witnesses to these episodes with Darwin so my fisticuffs ended at Harrison Township School.

Lesson Learned: Aggressiveness Has Its Place and Do Not Back Down From a Bully

As witness to my budding adolescence and obvious immaturity, I recall an incident in the music room at Harrison. After a gentleman by the name of Bill Schmalfeldt, a fellow Butler graduate, had left our school for greener pastures, he was replaced by a quiet and somewhat introverted musician named Ralph Kem. Bill, as I recall gave our very small high school band some recognition by doing very well in the various band contests around the state. He would later lead Southport High School in Marion County to the top level in high school band performance. Bill Schmalfeldt really supported us budding athletes while Ralph Kem did not.

Mr. Kem seemed to have disdain for us budding athletes and was somewhat condescending since we didn't seem to have an interest in his area—music. For some reason our class had gathered in the music home room which was Mr. Kem's exclusive territory.

No one had bothered to put away or, even fold up, the many music stands which were all around the room. Bored and tempted, a group of us proceeded to disassemble the music stands. I quickly discovered the main upright, which held the sheet music in place for the musician, made a great hollow tool for shooting almost anything that would fit into it.

We made "spitballs" and tried it out. Finally, one of my friends suggested that we target the group of girls who were sitting some two or three rows in front of us but with an open corridor to their backs. I lined up a shot and fired away. Suddenly a shriek came from Pat Hargis who was seated in the middle of the row of girls. I am not sure why she became our target but later on she would become my first relationship with the opposite sex. Well, Mr. Kem didn't take it lightly, and I think it must have required a visit to the Principal's Office.

Lesson Learned: Appreciate the Interests of Others and Grow Up

When I was in the eighth grade we had a new classmate named Lucille Green. At this point in our maturation process we were just beginning to notice the girls were starting to become women. Lucille was beautiful and seemed rather refined. She was not an extrovert by any measurement but we attributed this to her being the new person on the block. Later on, we found out that she had lost most or all of her immediate family in a tornado which had hit the other side of Delaware County the last spring. I can't remember how long Lucille stayed with us although she apparently was in a temporary living arrangement when she started the eighth grade with us.

Lesson Learned: Life Has Its Tragedies and the Opposite Sex Can be Beautiful

A friend of mine, John Patrick Drayer, who was two years my senior and the same age and a classmate of brother John's, spent his freshman year at McKinley Junior High School. At this time the Junior High Schools in Muncie included the seventh, eighth an ninth grades as a sort of middle school in today's terms. John Patrick was somewhat reserved and a smooth operator in those days. I am fascinated by a couple of his anecdotes of the time. John Patrick also would pay me a complement which I shall remember to my last day. In research for this writing effort, among other things John volunteered "I was also a team mate of the author, probably the best player in terms of ability to ever play for Harrison Township." So, while I'll always cherish this observation I am sure others would disagree, myself included.

The first involves John Patrick's compassion and sensitivity for the underprivileged. I still marvel about and have deep respect for John Patrick. It seems that as a freshman at McKinley he befriended a minority student. He learned to help his fellow man whenever possible.

John Patrick noticed a young minority student who would wonder around the cafeteria during lunch period but not eating lunch. So he asked this young man if he had any money for lunch. He did not. So John Patrick bought his lunch for several weeks. John Patrick says they had an "A" and a "B" lunch line with the "A" line being served a full course of a meat entrée, vegetables, fruit and dessert. The "B" line served soup, sloppy joes and a drink. Come to think of it that seems to mirror our menus at Harrison.

The "B" line cost was 25 cents. I remember 30 cents as the last price at Harrison. Some of our students would help with lunch and get their meals free of charge. Apparently, this young minority at McKinley did not have this option. John Patrick and his friend would eat at the "B" station line since John Patrick's budget wouldn't cover two line "A:" lunches. John Patrick says he always thought that two lunch lines discriminated against the "poor kids".

He says that he and his minority friend were the only mixed race kids in the cafeteria. Some, but not all, of the students looked down on them although not all of the students felt this way by any means. John Patrick never really gave a damn what they thought. This was the early 1950's. John Patrick was a trailblazer. I am glad that he came to Harrison the next year and became one of my friends.

Lesson Learned: Support and Help the Underprivileged

John Patrick's other revelation was rather humorous at least in retrospect. John was a new student as a freshman and registered as Pat Drayer. He had always gone by Pat previously since his full name was John Patrick Drayer. So, he completed his entry questionnaire as Pat Drayer.

John (Pat) was scheduled for a physical education class and on the first day as he bounded down the stairs into the dressing room to change into his gym togs, he was confronted by a group of half dressed and screaming freshman girls. Completely startled, John (Pat) quickly retreated to the Principal's office to ask what was happening. They quickly admitted that they had assumed that "Pat" was a female and had enrolled him in the freshman girl's gym class. That was the last time that Pat was Pat as he quickly became John Drayer. I never asked Pat why he didn't fake it, at least for a little while.

Lesson Learned: Details Can be Important

John Patrick also reminded me of how much more difficult it is to go through adolescence today than it was in the 1950's. He mentioned that we had never heard of marijuana and couldn't even spell it. He was so right. About the only substances around were tobacco and alcohol. He laughs heartedly as he recalls eight guys splitting a six pack of beer. "No one even had a full beer" he muses. Even so, that reminds me of a great friend and classmate, Leroy "Greg" Gregory, who was unceremoniously dismissed from our undefeated and tournament championship eighth grade basketball team for smoking. To this day Greg says he doesn't recall this although all of his contemporaries clearly remember this. In fact, Harold Keller, who was cut from the team earlier, was selected to replace Greg. Harold went on to play successfully for the Daleville Bronchos, another Delaware County School.

Lesson Learned: Growing Up Today has More Temptations

Chapter Twelve

Mrs. Heeter/Mrs. Carter

Times were certainly different back then. One of the best teachers I was fortunate enough to have guide me back then was Mrs. Barbara Heeter. We were fortunate to have other fine teachers at our small school. Of course, it didn't hurt that we were located in the same county as Ball State University which first made its name as Ball State Teachers College. Many young graduates would stay in the area after their undergraduate work to work on post graduate degrees or to help support a mate who was still doing undergraduate work.

Mrs.Heeter notes, things did change some over the period of years that she served as an educator. For instance, she makes note of the recent time, before dress codes came about, when she was forced to discuss dress codes with girls who were wearing spaghetti straps and some would have bare midriffs. So she talked to some of her students about the times and places when this type of dress was fine and when it should be avoided. She asked, "Would you wear a bikini to church?" A boy in the back of her classroom retorted, "Mrs. Heeter, if you had my Mom's figure you would". So that settled it in the minds of these youngsters. And, it is indelibly etched in the minds of all who were there.

Lesson Learned: In Cross Examination, Attorney's Never Ask a Question Unless they Know the Answer, So Remember That

Another example of Mrs. Heeter's experiences in the classroom in her later years of teaching, was when a student sitting right in front of her, asked to go to the restroom. Before she could respond, the student tossed her cookies. It was later discovered that the student had orange vodka for breakfast. This was a first period class. Mrs. Heeter resolved then and there, to learn more about her students lives away from school.

Lesson Learned: Holistic is Better

Earlier in Mrs. Heeter's teaching experiences, she confesses that she had to paddle the Principal's son. She was filled with trepidation and scared to leave the school building that evening. Nothing was said about the incident until the last day of school when the Principal said to Mrs. Heeter, "Eddie behaved after you paddled him. I am sure he needed it". This was 1946 when paddling and such discipline were permitted.

Lesson Learned: Rules are for Everyone

My most vivid and positive memory of Mrs. Heeter was our eighth grade English class. This was a grammar class, no literature to relieve our grammar anxieties. No escaping. Our grammar needed major development. She drilled us on nouns, verbs, adjectives, adverbs and we learned the purpose of conjunctions in our language. We also dealt with prepositional phrases, verb tenses and the need for their consistency and even the need to make our pronouns agree with their antecedents. We did this by learning the tools of sentence diagramming. She drilled us and drilled us. She was great at this. I struggled at first but eventually caught on to the point of being comfortable with all this. It would serve me well later on as my life unfolded.

Lesson Learned: Work Hard and Listen to Those Who Know

This would be incomplete without mentioning that Mrs. Heeter's husband was none other than Bob Heeter, a very successful basketball coach who would have many years of success in leading the Muncie

Southside Rebels after that school opened in the early 1960's. Brother John would later become the Athletic Director there where he served for some 23 years.

And, oh, Mrs. Heeter did find out who put the snake in her desk.

Lesson Learned: Mrs. Heeter was a Great Teacher

Mrs. Barbara Carter

Another of my favorite teachers was Barbara Carter although I certainly did nothing in her presence that would have illustrated any academic acumen at that time. Mrs. Carter, an attractive, bright, small in stature, and enthusiastic teacher of our freshman biology class, would find that I never had an answer when she called on me during class. You see, biology was somewhat like math for me, if you didn't read your assignments you simply didn't have the answers.

This class was assigned the freshman side of the high school assembly room. This was a pretty large room and even had upper classmen on the other side of the room that were in their free periods. We all had one or two of these free periods each day. To my embarrassment, my brother John was on the other side of the assembly room and was witness to all of my failures as Mrs. Carter called on me.

John got into me over this but I never seemed to be motivated to keep up in this class or any other class for that matter. John always seemed to do all his homework and more. He even vowed to read every book in our library, small as it was. He probably did so. For me, the library was a way to escape the assembly room and socialize. I guess I never figured it out until much later when I was working a couple of jobs to support my wife and three children and attending Ball State full time. I did find that by doing your homework you could do very well even in a college setting.

Lesson Learned: If You Can, Get Your Priorities Straight Early

Mrs. Carter, with her intelligence and adroit leadership also served as our librarian. Her husband, Gordon, was a Harrison Township graduate in 1948, a fact I didn't take note of until much later in life. Gordon also had his sheepskin from Purdue University, the agricultural and engineering school up the road in Lafayette.

As freshmen, Mrs. Carter traveled to Chicago for two days with our biology class. This was an annual excursion which she says she enjoyed as much as her students. In addition to going to the museums and International Livestock Exchange, we went to one of the first viewings of East of Eden. This was the first of three major films in which our neighbor from Fairmount, James Dean, would star. He was magnificent and it was a touching story of family dysfunction. He would later star in Rebel without a Cause and Giant before meeting his untimely demise in a tragic sports car accident.

Thanks to Mrs. Carter for having broadened our perspective of the real world. Mrs. Carter notes that many of us were experiencing our first big city and staying in a hotel. That was probably true in my case although I am not sure. She was a master of new experiences for us.

Lesson Learned: There's a Big Wonderful World Out There, So Get into It

I also remember Mr. Penrod, our outstanding Principal, calling in Spencer Campbell, Tom Robbins and me, and inviting all of us to travel to Purdue University with Mrs. Carter's husband Gordon, and a day of learning about this great Midwestern University. Well, I could understand the invitation to both Spencer and Tom but was surprised that I was included since I had done nothing of note in Mrs. Carter's biology class.

Both Spencer and Tom went on to have outstanding professional careers. Spencer ended up as a NASA scientist and Tom as an optometrist. I must have been a late bloomer since I was 26 before I earned a bachelor's degree and 33 when I had my MBA from Butler University in Indianapolis. That trip to Purdue must have made the right impression although I had not earned it in my view. It still seems as the nexus to my educational efforts after I gained some maturity.

Lesson Learned: If Once a Slacker, You Can Recover

Mrs. Carter says she still remembers having me in her biology class. I had hoped that she wouldn't. She remembers our games on the small Harrison basketball court although she would take a break from her teaching duties when I was a junior to start her family. In 1962 she would return and stay in the school corporation until retirement in 1997. Some forty years of leadership for which her students should be eternally grateful.

In remembering the circumstances of the day, Mrs. Carter describes it like this. "As a small township school, pre-television days, school activities played an important part in community life. I remember that most rode the bus since few students had a car of their own and few parents felt compelled to drive their kids to school. Parents came to PTA meetings and all other events at the school....after all it was the center of social life in addition to attending one of the seven churches that were in the township".

And Mrs. Carter was not one to shirk her volunteer duties. She would recall spending some fifteen straight hours in preparing for the fall school carnival. This was a major fund raising effort for the annual senior trip to Washington DC and New York. That was a major crowning of the students high school days. Not so today as most students have traveled extensively prior to graduation either as virtual travelers or in reality.

She also recalls other fund raising efforts including the selling of candy and cokes at high school basketball games. Due to the ingenuity of those before us, the soda cans would be iced down in a livestock watering tank in the afternoon prior to a game. Business always seemed to be quite good. After the game, the mess had to be mopped up, usually by some of the boys that had just played in the game.

Mrs. Carter went on to trump her recent observations by saying, "Due to the size of the school most teachers knew the entire family and understood something about the home life. This situation gave an entire school a certain 'family feeling' that isn't often experienced in today's society. I'm sure many students back then met with the old 'a spanking at school meant another one at home'. Teachers never considered ending up in court because some parent felt their child had been wrongly disciplined."

Boy, those were the good old days where you learned your lessons both from your teachers and your parents. They knew that model behavior was not a function of being your best friend but from guidance and discipline. These were the days before the mechanical joystick. There were no facades. You were what you did.

Mrs. Carter is gracious in mentioning that both John and I, not to the exclusion of the many other successful students that hailed from this small country school with a limited curriculum, had enjoyed some degree of success in our professional lives. Thanks Mrs. Carter and if I had it to do all over again I would read my biology assignments.

Lesson Learned: Here is Another Outstanding Teacher

Chapter Thirteen

High School Athletics
Baseball

"*Gib, let me tell you* about high school and our athletic pursuits." Gib couldn't wait to tease me about my embellishments.

Baseball

Our high school years resulted in two championships. There should have been more but injuries and immaturity would get in our way. Over our four years of high school competition we would win 58 of 86 games or a 67.4% winning percentage. When we started our summer league as a freshman we had an outstanding and experienced catcher in Sophomore Dean Campbell who was the third of five Campbell boys.

Both of Dean's older brothers, Larry and Wayne, had been outstanding athletes in both baseball and basketball. Larry ended up as a freshman starting guard on Ball state University's basketball team. Wayne would be a regular with Ball State's baseball team. So, the linage was there and Dean was a very smart cookie. Before the season was too far along, Dean was moved to third base and served mostly as our best pitcher. He was not large but was a flame thrower who had the quickest hard slider I can remember. And I remember all the good ones. I had begun my high school career at first base, a position I had never played before. But Coach

Boggs seemed to have expert intuition to move his guys around until he found just that right combination.

Freshman

During this, our first summer, we won a respectable eight games while coming up short on six occasions. Two of these encounters were by a single run. With all the underclassmen we were playing regularly, that wasn't too bad. We started by losing our first three games; Eaton, Royerton and then DeSoto. We would finish with a flourish, winning four of our last five games. We lost our final game in the championship playoff game to champion Selma.

It was a season of finding ourselves and our best positions. It is noteworthy that we reversed one of those first three losses, whacking DeSoto in our first playoff game by a mere 20 to 1.We ended up losing in the championship game so we were runners up as I just indicated. We had found our rightful positions with Dean pitching and, me, Johnny Hoosier behind the plate. Brother John, always a very dependable bat, ended up with a .444 batting average. Again, we had finished second best as playoff runners up.

The fall season of our freshman year was a setback from our summer league showing. We would win only three times while coming up short on five occasions. Four of those losses would come by two runs, one of those in extra innings.

One loss was of particular concern. This disappointment was accentuated by the fact that I had thrown the ball well over the head of our second and third basemen to allow Yorktown to come from behind and tie the score. They would win in nine innings.

I clearly was the reason for this loss. I just didn't learn to set my feet before I let it fly. And, with all that velocity, it wasn't a stretch to see the ball sail into the outfield. Close but it still goes on the loss side of the ledger. So, go figure, with a little more we could have very well ended up at seven wins and a single loss. We didn't , however. John still ended up with a respectable .392 batting average. I had settled in as the regular catcher despite the Yorktown game with Dean as our best flinger.

Sophomore

As a sophomore in the summer of 1955, we would win ten and lose three, finishing second best. We were blown out by the Royerton Redbirds in the playoffs, whom we had bested earlier during the season's regular schedule, 8 to 4. We had the better of Muncie Burris, Daleville, DeSoto, Yorktown, Cowan, split two games with Gaston, beat Center, Albany, and Selma. The only team we hadn't beaten during this season was Eaton as we lost 3-1. At this point I was the regular catcher as Dean was clearly the class of our pitching core. Another good pitcher was a classmate of mine, Mark Pitzer, a tall, slendor southpaw, whose submarine delivery brought the ball in from first base. Even though his velocity was, at best, batting practice speed, other teams had significant trouble hitting Mark since they obviously had never seen anything like a pitcher coming in from first base.

We started with a flourish, winning our first five games. In the opener, against Muncie Burris, Dean had 12 strikeouts. Keep in mind there are only 21 outs in these seven inning contests. I caught and John tripled in the winning run for a 2 to 1 victory.

We would lose our sixth game to Gaston by a score of 5 to 3. We would later avenge this loss in the first of our two playoff games by winning 6 to 2. We were 9 and 2 going into the playoffs, having paid back Yorktown for my throwing debacle last fall as a freshman by squeaking by them 4 to 3.

Alas, it was not to be as we lost our second playoff game to Royerton, having beaten them 8 to 4 earlier in the season. John would settle for a .314 batting average. I can't tell you what I did at the plate, but think it was respectable, except for my senior year I can say I batted .409 and sure handed Tom Robbins finished a thousandth or two higher and won the batting trophy. They must have had empathy for me since both Tom and

I were awarded batting trophies. Regrettably, I never kept any statistical records on anything. This is quite a departure from later years when statistical linear regression would become a fascination of mine.

In the fall of this sophomore year we were champions. I enjoyed this immensely since John was our leading hitter at .429 and played mostly as a top defensive centerfielder.

Our first game was a 9-0 whitewashing of the Center Spartans. I caught and Dean Campbell had eleven strikeouts while pitching a two hitter. John went one for two with a double. Our next game resulted in a second consecutive shutout with our submarine pitcher, Mark Pitzer, allowing six hits in an eleven to zero victory over Daleville. We were perfect in the field and had 14 hits as I caught. John had four hits in five at-bats including a triple and double.

We went on to defeat Yorktown 5-3 with Dean pitching and me behind the plate. Dean was a smart one as I've already mentioned. He repeated shook off the fastball and would pitch all hard sliders to Yorktown's leading hitter, a young man by the name of Gary Flick, who had previously hit a couple over the fence when I insisted on the high hard one. Dean struck Flick out from that point on as he couldn't hit that hard breaking pitch.

We then proceeded to win three more by a single run, defeating Selma 7-6, and then Eaton 4-3,and finally Cowan, 2-1. Against Selma, our small but the best pound for pound infielder all star, Phil Glaze, had a home run and double to lead our attack. Phil is best known as a member of the Delaware County Athletic Hall of Fame for his softball exploits following his high school career. He also, is known to have driven his Dad's John Deere tractor to practice as a freshman. And this wasn't a short distance as he lived a few miles from our high school.

We then won over Eaton with John scoring the winning run in the eighth inning. Against Cowan, we waited until the bottom of the last inning to score our winning run. I did the catching with Dean and Mark doing most of the flinging. Following this we won a slugfest over DeSoto, 17 to 10. The good news is that we banged out fifteen hits during this affair.

Phil Glaze had four hits including two doubles. Tom Robbins, our sure handed shortstop who would later have an outstanding career as an optometrist, banged out three hits.

We, at this point, were 7 and 0, and with one remaining game at our neighbor Gaston, who trailed us by a single game at 6-1. This game brings back some memories and not all good. As we trailed in the top of the last inning we were faced with our first loss with only three outs standing between us and that first defeat.

As the tying run came lumbering home, the plate Umpire Harry Shelby, was clearly out of position to see this close play. Although the runner clearly touched the plate prior to the catcher applying the tag Harry called him out.

He just couldn't see it. He was to the first base side of the plate with the catcher between him and our runner. Earlier I referred to the quiet confidence of Coach Boggs who never seemed to raise his voice, well......this time he was justifiably enraged and charged out to Harry Shelby and confronted him. Harry sure got his ears filled up and Coach Boggs, I think, picked up the 130 pound Harry before Coach restrained himself. Coach denies picking Harry off the ground so it must have been the turbulence of Coach's verbal lashing that picked old Harry off the ground. Harry deserved it.

Of all the times to blow a call! We lost, 7 to 6. Harry would soon not be accepted by Coach for any of the games he would coach in his illustrative career.

The next day, we would face Gaston in a playoff game since we were now both 7 and 1. We would play on a neutral diamond at Yorktown. This game should have become know as "Harry's Folly".

The morning of this playoff game I found that my catcher's hand was swollen and so sore that it hurt immensely even to the touch. I had caught every inning of every game during this fall season. How could I catch seven more innings with this problem? I couldn't even grip the bat let alone catch those hard balls from Dean Campbell. Well, we ended up wrapping my hand with a thick sponge and I played third base for the first time with Dean catching and Mark pitching the first five innings.

Because Dean was our marquee pitcher, he came in for the last two innings and I caught. Man those pitches got my attention. I don't recall a very successful day at the plate since I couldn't grip the bat properly. Jerry Fuson, grandson of our township trustee Vernon Fuson, short in stature but with a good bat, would go two for three at the plate. John also contributed a couple of hits to the cause.

After all this, and no Harry Shelby, we won the championship over Gaston by a score of 4 to 0. We were the best in the County. It felt very good. And John was part of it too.

This group of boys had won ten games the previous summer only to be upset in the playoffs. It was basically the team that had won eight games in the summer of 1954 when I was a freshman and we were just beginning to find our best lineup and had ended as runners up in the play offs. The regulars on this championship team included Mark Pitzer, Brother John, Bob Colter, the one with élan, who later would become principal at Harrison after it was converted to a middle school, Jerry Fuson, Dean Campbell, Phil Glaze, Tom Robbins, Dick "Trace" Brown who had thrown out runners from his fight field position after they lined clean singles to him, and myself as catcher.

This reiteration would be totally incomplete without mentioning our secret weapon. His name was/is Jeff Clements. Of course, you would not have known it if you would have run into Jeff on the street. You say; why is that? Well it is simply because Jeff, as a freshman and sophomore was barely five feet tall. And, he could swing the lumber too.

There were a number of occasions in those close games when Coach Boggs, in his wisdom, would send Jeff up to pinch hit. Jeff never let us down. He always got his base on balls. Crouching from his short stature so that his stance barely brought him up the opposing catcher's head even as the catcher was in his catching stance, he destroyed many a pitcher's concentration. That is probably a major reason we were able to pull out all those one run victories. Jeff was an outstanding weapon.

Harrison Wins County Baseball Title

Harrison Cardinals Baseball Champs 1955-56

Front row L to R: W. Clements., D. Addison, J. Clements, B. Carpenter, W. Lee. Second row: R. Wray, R. Murphy, M. Pitzer, J. Wray, S. Campbell, B. Colter. Third row: Coach Robert Boggs, J. Fuson, D. Campbell, P. Glaze, Principal L. Cline, L. Bailey, T. Robbins, R. Brown, Asst. Coach H. Platt

Photograph furnished courtesy of the Star Press

Junior

As the summer of 1956 came upon us Coach Boggs was faced with finding his best lineup again. We had lost John and Jerry Fuson to graduation along with our best pitcher, Dean Campbell to Muncie Central. Dean would play both basketball and baseball for the Bearcats during his senior year. But we still had six returning regulars from the previous fall's championship team. Plus, all the non-regulars. But, we were faced with finding a new order for our lineup. Only Coach Boggs could do this.

Without belaboring Dean's departure to Muncie Central, its genesis surely came from what had happened to Dean, John and I at the outside basketball court just outside the Muncie Field House. We would occasionally go there to trade baskets with some of the Bearcats and other post high school netters during the summer. Once while doing this, Bearcat Coach Jay McCreary approached John and I, to test our interest in moving over to the Bearcats.

He was probably thinking of a "double header" since both John and I were there. Of course, we stayed with our friends at good old Harrison Township. Dean, and his family, would later move from Harrison Township to Muncie where he would legitimately be eligible for immediate competition.

Yes, there was some recruiting going on at the time. Shortly after winning the eighth grade basketball championship against all the Muncie schools, I was approached on transferring to Wilson Junior High as a freshman. I would have entered Muncie Central as a sophomore and been oriented with my class as a potential Bearcat. I didn't bite of course.

During the summer of 1956, we would win eleven games, lose two, and win the summer baseball championship again. One of the high lights for me, personally, was to toss a no hitter against DeSoto midway in the season. This was my second no hitter to go along with an earlier one for the Sertoma Club in the City League. We would prevail over Yorktown 3 to 1 in the final game. I would go 2 for 3 at the plate with the telling blow being a triple to knock in the winning runs.

One of my friends would tell me afterward that the Yorktown fielders kept telling the Yorktown left fielder to back up when I came to the plate. Fortunately, he did not and I was able to send one flying over his head. By the time he had retrieved the ball and returned it to the infield I was at third base and we were leading 3 to 1. Coach Boggs had inserted me at second base for this game. I had played every position except second base during my previous tenure at HHS.

I recall committing and error when, with a man on first base, a grounder was sent out to our sure handed shortstop, Tom Robbins. As I drifted to second base for the force out, I could think of nothing except getting a double play. Well, my anxiousness led me to cross second base before Tom got the ball to me. The runner was safe and although I threw a hard strike to our first baseman it was a tie so both runners were safe. I don't think I ever played second base again. My teammates were probably lucky that I didn't.

Shortly after this summer championship, I was confronted, for the first time, with my physical mortality. Well morbidity is probably the correct term. One day while at work, preparing to make supplies deliveries for my restaurant employer, I suddenly had a shortness of breath and a pretty healthy sized pain in my right chest. Unable to relieve it, I visited the doctors' office directly across Madison Street from the drive-in restaurant of my employer.

I was sent directly to Ball Memorial Hospital where I would stay for nine days with a collapsed lung. It was caused by a virus according to the medical gurus. Officially it was called a 75% pneumothorax and had occurred spontaneously. Needless to say, I was not prepared for the unexpected occurrence. This deal would prevent me from playing in the fall baseball league until the very last two games of the year. And, I would play with no previous practice or conditioning.

We ended the season at four wins and four losses and out of the championship race. After sitting on the sidelines for the first six games we were at two wins and four losses. I did play the last two games which we did win against lesser opponents.

I even tried to pitch in the first game back, at least for a couple of innings. I had no velocity and the natural screwball was gone because of the lack of speed. It was a good thing we were playing lesser opponents. The only later fall out from this was in our first basketball game of the season where we would lose in overtime to Eaton, 60 to 58. During the overtime, I would experience for the second time, this pain in my right chest area. I will deal with this later when we comment on our basketball endeavors.

Senior

As a senior during the summer baseball season, I would experience a devastating injury to my pitching arm during our playoff game with

Muncie Burris at the Ball State University diamond. It was the first batter in the first inning for Muncie Burris when, after getting two strikes on the batter, I tried a little curve ball and the batter swung and missed. That was good!

But.............something had popped in my elbow area. I both felt it and heard it. Being young and not one to bow out so early in a game, I continued through the first inning with no damage on the scoreboard. By the second inning, I knew something was wrong and afterward told our new coach Hall Platt that something was wrong with my arm. He didn't react until the fourth or fifth inning when he finally relented and moved me to third base. By that time I couldn't even throw an occasional runner out. Muncie Burris sensing my dilemma, started bunting to third base in the last inning. I couldn't even throw underhanded by that time. We lost.

The next week, in a game with Muncie Central, my arm was as large as my waist. Admittedly my waist was a little smaller in those days so it is not a great stretch to envision this. We beat the Bearcats 18 to 3 that day and my duty was to try to pinch hit in the latter stages of the game and found it was impossible to swing the bat with any authority. It was so painful. To this day, it is impossible to straighten that right elbow.

A little surgery would have been in order if it happened in today's world of orthopedic surgery. I know, since I have an artificial hip, injured while jogging at age 63 in the cold November winds in Minnesota. But this was the 1950's.

In retrospect, I think that the damage was done after the initial injury since Coach Platt wouldn't remove me until several innings later. I have not forgiven him for that. I never pitched again and stayed at third base. There is a noticeable gap between the two bones connecting my forearm to my bicep. And, at one point I had been approached by a business owner who had connections with the Chicago Cubs. He had wanted to set up a tryout with the Cubs. Alas, it was not to be. Dang it!

During the fall of my senior year, we would finish the season at 5 and 3. I played all but the last game since I had been involved in an altercation with some subhuman testosterone infested hoods from Muncie who accosted my friends and I and I took a couple of brass knuckles to my eye area. My right eye would be closed for a week or so and I sat out my final high school baseball game at Gaston.

As the Cardinals struggled, and finally lost, my friend from Gaston, Jim Delaney, who had been with me the night before during the altercation, and I, stood along the sidelines watching play. An older gentleman turned to my friend, Jim, and said, "I thought they had this great pitcher." Jim quickly responded, "you are looking at him' as he turned to me. What a disastrous way to end a baseball career. It is noteworthy that Coach Boggs, now at Selma High School, would go on to win the championship this year and the following three years.

Although I would later play in the Eastern Indiana Baseball league for a couple of teams, that was essentially it for me in the great game of baseball as I finally got it and focused on college and my young family.

Chapter Fourteen

High School Athletics Basketball

Overall

In high school, basketball was a steady progression of improvement. Overall, including our eighth grade year in which we were undefeated, we would win 67.0% of our games. There was steady improvement in this winning percentage going from 35.0% (100% as eighth graders) as a freshman to 52.2% as a sophomore, 62.5% as a junior to our best year, 92.0% as a senior. While in the eighth grade our very young varsity had won only two games. As a freshman we prevailed in seven contests, twelve as a sophomore, then fifteen as a junior and finally as a senior we won twenty-three games. We were sectional runners up to Muncie Central as a junior and senior and were percentage champions during the last year.

Freshman

The 1954-1955 basketball season was greeted with higher anticipation than the previous year when the Cardinals would finish 2 and 17. Three starters returned including my brother John , who led all scorers the previous year with 217 points, tall center Ed Townsend and a cagey guard Jack Sayre. Dee Clevenger and Larry Hargis were reserves and were also back. The only two seniors were Townsend and Sayre.

A local sports columnist, Ed Satterfield described it this way. "Coach Boggs is especially pleased with six freshmen on the roster. While these youngsters are not counted on to carry the varsity banner for at least a year or two, don't be surprised if they leave their niche in the Harrison Hall of Fame. As eighth graders, these youngsters breezed through the county grade school tourney a year ago. Three of them are six footers and a fourth stands 5-11. Coach Boggs wants to keep them together as a unit, which means they will receive valuable training this season in second-team competition."

Another sports columnist, John Farrell, had this to say. "So, all in all, it looks like the Cardinals are getting ready to forsake the cellar, and in a few years make it especially rough on the other county basketball teams."

So this was our send off. We would leave the cellar but would finish only 7-13. Not good enough! One of our problems was the taller and more experienced boys from Selma who would prevail in the county tourney and thump us a couple of times during the year.

After about eight games on the junior varsity, and a 6-2 record, Coach came to my last period algebra class and called me out in the hall. He explained that he was separating me from my classmates and moving me to the varsity. He further explained that he expected me to keep everything in perspective and not to become too enamored with myself. I think I made a couple of dumb comments before I realized that I should only be listening. We played county powerhouse Yorktown that evening with their dominating center Modie Beeman.

I mistakenly assumed that my participation would be in a backup roll. Not true. As we prepared to tip off, I was sent in to play the pivot and jump center against Modie.

Needless to mention, we got our inexperienced butts kicked. What an introduction to the varsity. Our next game against Daleville in their new and large goal house, I would start at guard. We lost that one too. From that point on my role was as a reserve, mostly to our tall center Ed Townsend. This was a learning year, although I found I could jump with most anyone regardless of the height deficit. After all, I was only 5-11 at the time.

This varsity team was lead by stalwarts, Jack Sayre, brother John , Dee Clevenger, tall Ed Townsend, and later on in the year Dean Campbell, our star pitcher and another sophomore Jerry Mifflin, a tall a slender lad with some intellectual talent which he would use later in his career. Jack, a small but smooth ball handler, would almost single handedly take care of neighboring Gaston by scoring 30 points in a 65-56 victory. He was amply supported by John who scored 19 points. This was the first victory over the Bulldogs since the 1950-1951 season. These two would repeatedly lead Harrison's scoring parade.

In retrospect, it was a year of building but I did miss my classmates who would dominate the reserve class through the next two years and win county championships. We, the varsity, would finish with 7 wins and 13 losses. Not so hot! But slightly better than the previous year's 2 wins and 17 losses. My brother John would lead all scorers with 279 points.

Harrison Cardinals, 1953-54

Back row L to R: G. Huffman, J. Sayer, M. Irwin, B. Brown, E. Townsend, L. Edwards, J Wray, D. Clevenger, L. Hargis, C. Nauman. Front row L to R: J. Nauman, Coach Boggs, R. Wray

Some of the 1954-55 Cardinals

Coach Bob Boggs

Brother John Wray
Junior

Dean Clevenger
Junior

Jack Sayer
Senior

Dean Campbell
Sophomore

Dick Brown
Sophomore

Ed Townsend
Senior

Ralph Wray
Freshman

Ballet on Hardwood

Cards in Action, 1954
Brother John goes for the score

Cards in Action
Brother John and Mike Irwin in action

Cardinal in Action 1954
Brother John Wray and Ed Townsend
surround Cowan's Bill Garrett

Photographs furnished courtesy of the Star Press

1954-55 Cardinals
Back Row L to R: H. Heistand, R. Brown, D. Clevenger, J. Drayer, J. Wray, E. Townsend, J Mifflin, R. Wray, D. Campbell, J. Sayer.
Front Row: R. Bailey, Coach Boggs, Principal L. Penrod, R. Campbell

Sophomore

The annual pre-season coverage of the Harrison Cardinals for the 1955-1956 year was labeled "Harrison Township Prospects Bright." Well that is some way to put us behind the eight ball. A total of nine games had been won in the previous two years. But only two seniors had left from a year earlier.

Sports columnist Ed Satterfield put it this way, "Harrison Township would like nothing better than to place a basketball title beside its baseball title in the school trophy case.

Indications are Coach Robert Boggs' Cardinals may soar high in the county cage realm this winter. Graduation losses were negligible and the team was beginning to hit a consistent stride when the curtain came down late in February."

"Harrison won seven and lost twelve in the 1954-55 campaign, which placed it tenth in the standing. However, the pea-green material ripened steadily after mid-season."

"Jack Sayre and Ed Townsend, a pair of regulars, were the only graduation losses. Eight others are back in the harness and the squad has been augmented by the addition of another performer who played regular at Cowan High School."

"Coach Boggs stated he would divide the squad into two sections this week. He intimated that the division would be rather hard to make, inasmuch as several of the younger athletes were showing unusual ability."

"Veterans include Dee Clevenger, Harold Heistand, John Drayer, John Wray, Dick Brown, Dean Campbell, Jerry Mifflin, and Ralph Wray. Clevenger, J.Wray and D. Campbell were starters last year and R. Wray, although only a freshman, was a part time regular."

"Jim Wininger, 5-7 junior, moved in from Cowan during the summer and may be a hard lad to keep out of the starting lineup. He did a bang-up job for John Harding's Blackhawks last year and could be the spark needed to generate a Harrison cage revival. 'I will have a strong bench' Boggs stated. 'This team will have a good balance, something which has been lacking in the past'."

"The Cardinals will not lack for rebounders, if the height situation can be taken as a criterion. Seven of the 23 net aspirants are at, or above, the six-foot measurement."

"Much of the talent is spread through the freshman-sophomore group, inasmuch as most of these boys of the Harrison team which took the county eighth grade tournament two years ago."

"J. Wray, a six foot senior, led the Cardinal scoring last year and will likely be a starter this fall. Heistand or Wininger are leading the race to succeed Sayre, while R. Wray and Drayer are battling for the position left vacant by Townsend's departure."

So here's the lineup:

Player
*Dee Clevenger, 5-10, 145, Sr.
*John Drayer, 5-9 ½, 147, Sr.
*Harold Heistand, 5-7, 156, Sr.
*John Wray, 6-0 ½, 158, Sr.
*Richard Brown, 5-8, 158, Jr.
*Dean Campbell, 5-8, 135, Jr.
*Jerry Mifflin, 6-1 ½, 140, Jr.
Don Bailey, 5-7, 132, Jr.
James Brown, 5-7, 150, Jr.
Bob Colter, 5-9 ½, 153, Jr.
Phil Glaze, 5-6, 125, Jr.
Jerry Thompson, 5-8, 132, Jr.
James Wininger, 5-7, 138, Jr.
*Ralph Wray, 5-11 ½, 159, Soph.
Spencer Campbell, 6-0 ½, 144, Soph.
Bruce Carpenter, 5-6, 132, Soph.
Wayne Clements, 5-3, 113, Soph.
Bill Long, 6-0, 143, Soph.
Robert Murphy, 6-2, 142, Soph.
Mark Pitzer, 6-0 ½, 157, Soph.
Tom Robbins, 5-7, 133, Soph.
Larry Bailey, 5-7, 115, Fresh.
John Murphy, 6-0, 137, Fresh.

*Lettermen

Another sports columnist, Dave Harrison, had his copy editor assign the headline to his offering on Harrison as "Harrison Ready to Settle Old Scores." The writer went on to say, "Better days are coming out at Harrison Township where Robert Boggs is ready to begin his fourth term at the helm of the Cardinal cage squad. An indication of the uphill climb of the Harrison athletic fortunes came recently when the school baseball team captured the county championship."

"Although Boggs isn't saying much—at least yet---it's clear that he feels his youngsters are capable of a first division finish in the county percentage race. "

"That would be quite a change from the last couple of winters when the Cardinals sagged to a last-place finish in 1953-54 and only one notch higher in 1954-55. The Harrison quintet of a year ago won seven and lost 13."

"Reason for Boggs' guarded optimism is the fact that he has eight experienced varsitymen, a promising crop of freshmen and sophomores and a transfer from Cowan all available for immediate action."

"Harrison is probably still a year or two away from being considered a "county power', but should be able to hold its own with veterans like Dee Clevenger, John Drayer, Harold Heistand, John Wray, Richard Brown, Dean Campbell, Jerry Mifflin and Ralph Wray. The entire group won monograms last season and only the first four named are seniors."

"Only personnel losses were Jack Sayre, whose 223 points was second-high on the team, and Ed Townsend, who dunked 169 for third high. Both departed via the diploma route."

"Clevenger and John Wray gathered 148 and 279 points respectively as regular forwards and seem assured of starting berths again. Dean Campbell, who popped 119, is the third regular back. He teamed with Sayre at the guard posts."

"Heistand or James Wininger, a junior transfer who earned a letter at Cowan during the 54-55 campaign, are regarded as the most likely prospects to assume Sayre's vacated back court position."

"Ralph Wray, who alternated with Townsend in the pivot slot during the later portion of the season, has been tapped for those duties again. He'll get help from Drayer."

"Boggs can't help breaking into a grin when he speaks of his second team. 'I'm looking forward to great things from that bunch,' he admits. 'Some of those freshmen and sophomores are apt to be playing varsity ball by Christmas if they show me enough'."

"The usually conservative Cardinal mentor has good reason to be enthusiastic. The current second-team won the county junior high tourney as seventh and eighth graders and played more outstanding ball last season."

So, we've been set up twice before the first tip off.

We started against Stoney Creek, a school which is probably the only smaller school that we played in terms of enrollment. It was at Farmland on a neutral floor. We ended up losing by three points after leading early in the contest. I recall a couple of errors near the end of this very close encounter. As I pulled up for an eight footer from the right side with seconds to go I saw Dee Clevenger right dead center under our basket with his defender behind him. Just drop a pass to Dee and it's an easy lay up with the possibility of a foul from his defender. Alas, a near perfect bounce pass deflected off Dee's hands and out of bounds it went. A major opportunity lost.

Shortly thereafter, we were in our full court press mode. As the opponents tried a long pass to my position as one of two front court defenders, it was easy to just step in front of the Stoney Creek player and intercept the pass. We still had a chance to pull this one out. It was not to be, as I dribbled into our end of the court the ball suddenly bounced very high and traveling was called. I do not recall that ever happening before or after. Must have been a flaw in the floor because we had one at home in about the same location although we never divulged this to any opponent.

I had blown our opportunity and was astonished as the mainstay of our opponents was gleefully clapping, laughing and pointing in my direction. I didn't need that but had learned a lesson in sportsmanship—never behave like that. Inevitably we lost our first game and shouldn't have. Dean Campbell scored 11 points, John had 15 and I was able to garner 12 despite the end of game errors. We are now 0-1.

Our next game was against power house Eaton with their tall line up of Jim Taylor and Jack Tapy. They had the best of us by eleven points on their home floor. I recall giving a head fake to Jack Tapy, about six inches taller than I at the time, and Jack went for it completely. He came all the way over my back and landed on his head. I thought he had hurt himself, possibly quite severely. Jack was OK and continued to dominate us on the boards.

My brother John would score 18 points but the game was a major step forward for us as Phil Glaze entered the game as a substitute and went on to lead us with 19 points. Phil was never permanently dislodged for his guard position until after he graduated. Inch for inch, Phil was simply the best. We are now 0-2.

Our third encounter would go our way overwhelmingly. We bested Center by a score of 83-55. My brother John would again lead us with 22 points, reserve John Drayer and slender Jerry Mifflin would both chip in with 14 and Phil Glaze, our new found back court star had 13. We are now 1-2.

We followed with an encounter with Daleville in which we found the basket for an astounding 106 points. That's not bad for as 32 minute encounter. Daleville also scored well with 68 points. Dean Campbell and Phil Glaze threw in 23 points apiece, and brother John chipped in with 17. We actually had six players with 9 or more points. So we are now 2 and 2. Not good enough considering our preseason publicity.

The last two games were history as we succumbed to eventual county champion Gaston by a score of 59 to 48. We sure needed some of those excess Daleville points. Again brother John would lead the way with 23 markers. We are now 2-3.

Our next encounter was against perennial power Royerton. We had them on our home court and bested them by a whopping 93-62. Phil Glaze offered up 21 points, slendor Jerry Mifflin and I both chipped in with 20, mostly off the offensive boards, and brother John countered with 17. We were now 3 and 3. Not good enough.

The county scoring parade came out at this point with brother John being first in the entire county, Phil Glaze as number seven, Dean Campbell as number nineteen and myself as number thirty, just two spots above the cutoff. Thirty-two cagers were listed.

Our next encounter was a loss to Cowan on their home court with its lack of glass backboards. They beat us good. I was able to throw in 13 counters and brother John 10. No other Cardinal broke the double figures in this one. Gosh, we're now less than .500 at 3 and 4.

We went down again against an experienced and taller Yorktown squad by twelve points. Dean Campbell had a breakout game with 25 counters and I, the only other Cardinal in double figures, followed with 11. EEK! We are now 3-5.

The county scoring parade would come out again twice during the month of December. The first one listed brother John as the number four scorer in the county, Dean Campbell as 17th, Phil Glaze as 18th and me, Johnny Hoosier, as number 27. A week later our positions showed John as number 2nd, Dean as 13th, Phil at 18th and me still number 27 of the thirty-two players listed.

In our last game of 1955, we went to Daleville and had the best of them 70 to 49. Brother John scored 27 markers and Dean Campbell chipped in with 16. We were now at 4-5. This is still not good enough at all.

We started the new year by besting DeSoto 75 to 41 at their goal house where the visitors dressing room was actually a second floor elementary classroom. Oh well it was still back in the 1950's. While it was not a particularly challenging game for us it did have some excitement. A husky forward for DeSoto, Jim Huffman, would liven things up by punching one of the referees. As I picked off a long rebound and drove hell bent up the floor toward our end of the court, Jim reached across and tried to swat the ball from me. He was standing still and I was moving quickly so he didn't have a chance to get the ball at all. Needless to say, the whistle blew and Jim was charged with a reaching in foul. As I stopped and turned to look behind me Jim was already confronting the whistle caller, suddenly his right fist came into the referee's face and chest. Huffman was thrown out of the game and never played again. So it wasn't entirely boring. Bob Colter scored 13, brother John and Dean Campbell had 10 and I chipped in with 12. We were now back at .500 and 5-5. This is still less than our expectations.

In our last encounter prior to the county tournament, we bested Selma 78-51 on our home court. Dean Campbell would garner 19 points, Jerry Mifflin 17 and I chipped in with 13 markers. We, at last, were over .500 at 6-5 and the county tournament stared us in the face.

We were listed as a dark horse for the tournament with Cowan, Gaston and Eaton being the favorites. We drew Royerton for our first encounter. We would prevail 55-51 after having bested them in our goal house earlier by 31 points. It was a tight game and I fouled out on a charging call with a little over 1 minute remaining. Phil Glaze would lead the way with 16 points and I would chip in with 15. Things seemed to be heading in the right direction as we were now 7-5.

In our semifinal game we would lose to eventual champion Gaston with their outstanding big man Phil Kibbey scoring 25 points against us. Phil would go on to play at Memphis State, the alma mater of his Coach Phil Hodson. We had lost by a score of 68 to 57. Phil Glaze would lead us with 18 points, with Dean Campbell getting 13 and brother John 12. Well we were going in the wrong direction again and were now 7-6.

We would face the champion Bulldogs again a week following the tourney. This time we would lose by a score of 61-54. Unacceptable. Dean would get 16 markers, Phil 14 and I had 10. Holy Moly we were now back at .500 at 7-7.

We followed by a trip to Mooreland in Henry County and, although we had five more field baskets, could not overcome the constant whistle blowing as Mooreland tallied 33 free throws. They had been handed 44 free throw attempts. Seemed a little unbalanced. Our favorite baseball umpire, Harry Shelby, was one of the whistle blowers. We would succumb 67-59. Dean Campbell had 23 markers and brother John garnered 15. Mooreland's tall and burley center couldn't get off the floor very much as I was able to block some of his turn around jumpers cleanly. We are now below .500 at 7-8.

The Delaware County scoring parade was again listed with brother John as number four, Dean Campbell as fifth, Phil Glaze as fifteenth and me pulling up the rear in 22nd position. There were approximately 156 roster holders on the thirteen teams in the county, excluding Muncie Burris and Muncie Central.

We traveled to Randolph County to face Ridgeville following the Moreland debacle. We started strong but would succumb to a deathly zone defense later in the game. We lost 51-47. Dean Campbell would garner 12 points and I chipped in with 11. We are now two games below breakeven at 7-9.

We faced Cowan, one of the pre-tourney favorites next. We dropped this one 92-66. Not much defense. This must have been why we focused on our own 1-2-2 zone so much later on as we started to get the message. Phil glaze had 20 points, brother John 17, and I had 13. This has got to stop. We are now 7-10.

Next was DeSoto at home. We prevailed by a score of 73 to 48. There was no Jim Huffman in this one. Dean Campbell netted 20 markers, Bob Colter 17, Mifflin 16 and I had 10. We are now 8-10.

We then beat Albany 76-65 in a home game. Dean Campbell bombed the nets for 27 points and Phil Glaze followed with 22. We are now 9-10.

We next busted Center 74-53 with Dean and Phil leading the way again with 22 and 18 points respectively. Hello .500 we are back again at 10-10.

As the Sectional stared in the face we were nothing more than a small school club with a .500 average. Well that may be but we were going to give it a run. We knew we were better than that 10-10 record. A number of games had gone the other way, some for the wrong reasons. Two in particular, the Moreland game with referee Harry and the Ridgeville game. My playing time had diminished in the later stages of the season primarily due to my immaturity and rules with the opposite sex which Coach Boggs had rightly imposed. So, the lesson learned this year was to buck up and follow all the rules in the future which I did. My playing time never diminished again, at least for this reason.

We took out DeSoto 69-49 in our first sectional encounter. Keep in mind that this one put us over .500 at 11-10 We next faced champion Gaston. We would win that one also, against all prognosticators, 57-44. Guess what, we are now 12 10.

We would lose the semi-final game to tall Eaton by a whopping score of 58-35. We were finished at 12-11. This record certainly is unimpressive but very well could have been 16-7. Although we had moved up to fifth in the standings, we couldn't wait for the next year.

1955-56 Cardinals

Seated: Glaze, R. Wray, Mifflin, J. Wray, Campbell. Standing: Beedle, Manager; Bob Boggs, Coach; Wininger, Drayer, Colter, Lowell Cline, Principal; Baily, Manager

Some of the 1955-56 Cardinals

Left, Coach Boggs. Right, Brother John Wray, Senior

Left, Phil Glaze, Junior
Right, Ralph Wray, Sophomore

Left, Dean Campbell
Right, Jerry Mifflin
both Juniors

Cards in Action 1955-56
Phil Glaze goes for the score (see ball),
Ralph Wray prepares to rebound
Bob Colter in background

Cards in Action 1955-56
Ralph Wray goes for a rebound

Photographs furnished courtesy of the Star Press

Junior Year

After last year's shortfall, when we lagged our press clippings until the very end off the season, we should have been more wary of the pre-season write ups for 1956-57. As we repeatedly stumbled early, we fell prey to the same phenomena as the previous year. We would close with a flourish, however, falling one game short of the Regional level in the state tournament.

Starting in late January, Coach Boggs in his wisdom, started Saturday practices and we ran and ran. And then ran some more. We would cross the gym floor at one end and climb the theater seat stairs to the very top row, run across the top row, then descend and run across the other end of the floor, cross it and jump to the side of the gymnasium stage by jumping to that level, run across the stage and jump down on the starting end of the floor. We never were in this great shape before and would never be so again. We could have played two 32 minute games and not have slowed a bit.

Bob Barnet, the prominent sports writer for the Muncie Star put it this way. "Harrison, a surprise team in the 1956 Muncie sectional, will open with five lettermen and what Coach Bob Boggs describes as fair prospects. If the Cardinals take off where they left off a year ago they may better that rating."

"In sectional competition the Redclads opened with a 68-49 romp over DeSoto, then eliminated Gaston, the county champion, in the second round, 57-44, before surrendering to towering Eaton 68-35."

"Of the six who played in that semifinals game, Boggs has all but guard Dean Campbell, whose family moved and who is a candidate for a place on the Muncie Central varsity."

Barnet had failed to mention that we had lost brother John, who was nursing an injury a year earlier in the sectional and had been one of our leading scorers for three years, and reserve John Drayer via graduation. So much for knowing your subject.

"Boggs, who is a Ball State graduate, expects to start Spencer Campbell, 6-1, and Ralph Wray, 6-0 ½ , at forwards, Jerry Mifflin. 6-2 ½, at center, and Phil Glaze and Butch Wininger, both 5-8, at the guard posts. Also around is Bob Colter, 5-11, who was a starter in the semifinals game."

"Campbell is a graduate of a Harrison reserve team that was good enough to win the county second-team tourney last season. So are Tom Robbins, a 5-8 ½ guard, and Bruce Carpenter, a 5-8 guard, both of whom are listed with the varsity."

"The Harrison varsity won 12 and lost 11 last year and as the record shows, was coming very fast at the close of the season. With his starters nearly intact, Boggs heads into a new season in pretty fair shape, although depth may be a problem unless the second-team graduates come through. Boggs makes it plain that the 12-man squad listed here is not definite, as changes may be made even before the season opens."

"Boggs insists that everybody on the Harrison schedule looks tough to him but picks Eaton, Gaston, Royerton, Cowan and Yorktown as the most dangerous his Redclads will be called on to face. The Redclads will get into action with a bang, meeting Eaton at Harrison in their opener on Nov.2."

"Harrison varsitymen got a taste of the heady brew of big-game victory last year. There is every reason to believe they will come back for more."

So, here's the lineup to start the season:

*Jerry Mifflin, c, 6-2 ½, 156, Sr.
*Bob Colter, f, 5-11, 157, Sr.
*Phil Glaze, g, 5-8, 140, Sr.
*Butch Wininger, g, 5-8, 142, Sr.
*Ralph Wray, f, 6-0, 160, Jr.
Spencer Campbell, c, 6-1, 152, Jr.
Bruce Carpenter, g, 5-8, 144, Jr.
Tom Robbins, g, 5-8 ½, 130, Jr.
Bob Murphy, f, 6-2, 150, Jr.
Bill Long, f, 6-2, 158, Jr.
John Ramsey, f, 6-1, 195, Jr.
Mark Pitzer, f, 6-2, 170, Jr.
John Murphy, c, 6-3, 151, So.
Larry Bailey, g, 5-10, 128, So.
Don Addison, g, 5-6, 120, So.
Rex Jackson, f, 5-8, 155, Fr.
Dick Humphries, g, 5-4, 120, Fr.
Jeff Gardner, f, 5-5, 130, Fr.
Joe Holmes, f, 5-9, 130, Fr.
Phil Drumm, f, 5-11, 163, Fr

*lettermen

Another sports writer, Dave Harrison, had his pre-season column labeled this way, "Bright Future for Harrison Cardinals." Well, here we go again. Is this another clippings jinx?

"Harrison's Cardinals, despite a modest 12-11 record, acquired a 'spoilers' reputation around Delaware County last winter by saving their best games for the county leaders."

"Perhaps their biggest single accomplishment was pulling the rug out from under Gaston, the county tourney champ, in a second-round sectional game. The Cardinals won that one, 57-44, avenging three previous defeats at the hands of the Bulldogs."

"With five of his first eight back, plus a flock on new prospects, Bob Boggs appears to have the makings of a squad which will create even greater mischief this year."

"Chief loss from the 1955-56 team was Dean Campbell, who has moved with his family into the city and is presently a candidate for the Muncie Central cage squad. A two-letterman, Campbell was Harrison's leading scorer last year with 321 points."

"Also gone, via the graduation route, are John Wray, No. three scorer, and substitute John Drayer." So Dave Harrison had done his research unlike Bob Barnet.

Most brothers do not have the luxury and euphoria of playing together as teammates. Some do. Like Bob and John Murphy, or Bob and Phil Boggs, and me, Johnny Hoosier playing with brother John. Both of the Boggs brothers said that playing with their talented brother was the highlight of their high school careers. I completely understand that since it was true for me also. John and I played together on two varsity quintets for Harrison. I am sure the Murphy boys would also agree.

"On the bright side, Boggs still has Phil Glaze and James (Butch) Wininger, a couple of 5-8 senior guards who possess lots of backcourt savvy. Both of them are excellent 'outside' shooters , particularly Glaze who pitched in 267 points as a junior."

"Three other lettermen---Jerry Mifflin (6-2 senior), Bob Colter (5-11 senior) and Ralph Wray (6-1 junior)---will give Harrison valuable experience up front. All three play pivot or center posts with near equal ability, although Wray usually jumps center."

"Boggs also has several good-looking prospects up from the reserve team which won the second team tourney last season. Several are pressing the five holdover lettermen for starting jobs."

"Spencer Campbell (6-1, junior) has been impressive in practice sessions and may win a starting berth at forward, while Tom Robbins (5-8, junior) and Bruce carpenter (5-8, junior) are keeping Glaze and Wininger on their toes at guard."

"Two others whom Boggs is keeping an eye on as varsity timber are Bob Murphy and Bill Long, a pair of 6-2 juniors."

"Boggs is starting his fifth year at Harrison and the former Selma and Ball State grad could wind up having his most successful season. With fair height, good speed, experience and a team which can 'hit', the Cardinals figure to stay close to just about everyone on the circuit."

So are we jinxed again? Would we have been better served without any pre-season publicity?

Our first encounter was against Eaton at home. Eaton had lost 6-5 Jim Taylor, one of the highest scoring centers in county basketball history, along with three other starters. So they weren't expected to produce a lot at the beginning of the season. Joe Hahn a 5-11 forward was the only returning starter. However, two reserves from the year before, Tony Rees and Bob Simmons were better than starters on a number of other county teams. Then it also was the beginning of varsity for Budge Hahn, brother of Joe, and Gary Clevenger, who would go on to win the county championship in their final year of competition. They were sophomores this year. So, we didn't know what to expect and even their presentation in the Muncie Star read simply, "Eaton Building; Seven Lettermen Gone." They were taking the low road.

I remember netting the tying field goal as regulation expired. It was an eight footer from the left side and was high off the glass but went cleanly through the nets. This had been a nip and tuck game throughout with Eaton leading after one, 8-7. We were in command at the half 20-18 and after three quarters 35-32. After regulation expired it was 49-49.

Both squads would pick up their scoring during the 5 minute overtime session. Handsome Bob Simmons would net seven for Eaton during the overtime session but Phil Glaze would knock in eight for us. Not enough help for Phil. I clearly recall being back on defense during overtime and having that sharp pain in my right chest. Should I ask for time out and tell Coach Boggs. Yes I should have but, you guessed it, I did not. I could hardly stand straight up. It was that lung that had collapsed the August before.

We lost 60-58 and it was too late to do anything. Phil would net 21 points and I would follow with 12. No other Cardinal scored more than 7. Oops, that's 0-1 in the win-loss column.

We went to Center High School for our second encounter. It was also our second overtime encounter of this young season. This time, however, we would prevail 63-59. Butch Wininger and Tom Robbins would both net 11 a piece for us with Mike Readnour scoring 26 for the Spartans. Mike would later go on to lead all county scorers and play for the Ball State Cardinals. Well, we are now 1-1.

So we now go to Daleville to pay a visit to the Bronchos. We were both 1-1 at this point. Although we won the battle of field goals 24-23, we trailed by six at the charity stripe. The Bronchos prevailed, 68-64. We had led at all stopping points prior to the final gun. Phil Glaze would throw in 19 points and Butch Wininger and I, 12 a piece. Crap, we are now 1-2 and the two losses are by 2 and 4 points. We should have won this one since we clearly had better athletes.

We would have a visit from our neighbor and defending county champ Gaston for our next encounter. Led by Phil Kibbey, Jerry Janney and Voyne Smith, first cousin of my first cousin Bernie Smith, they were awesome. We would see Gaston hit the nets at an amazing .478 rate.

We would come up short 70-62. The Bulldogs had paid us back for the defeat in last years' sectional. Butch Wininger would lead us with 16 points and Phil Glaze and slender Jerry Mifflin would chip in with 14 each. The Bulldogs were lead by Kibbey with 17, Voyne Smith had 16 and Jerry Janney followed with 15. Geez, we now looking like last year and are only 1-3.

So let's now go over to Royerton and set things straight. After all we bested them twice last year. It was not to be. The headline read, 'Royerton wins Thriller." The Redbirds prevailed 54-50. That's our fourth loss of four points or less. We were tied with less than two minutes remaining but couldn't pull it put. Things are not looking good since we are now 1-4.

We now were paid a visit by the Cowan Blackhawks with their outstanding coach John Harding. Coach Boggs experimented and started all juniors in this one. After all, we were supposed to reach the upper echelon this season and had started 1-4, winning only in overtime and losing the four by four points or less. We weren't beating anyone's chops at this point. So Coach had to mix it up in an effort to find something that worked better. I was spared and started as I was a junior. He would do the same the next game against Yorktown but I was not spared and sat on the bench as the game started. We scored well and bested the Blackhawks 84-74. But what about the defense? Phil Glaze came off the bench to lead us with 21 points, Tom Robbins and Bob Colter would follow with 12 and Spencer Campbell had 11. Alas, I only had 9 but we had finally won again. We are now 2-4 and most certainly not what we had anticipated.

The next week it was Yorktown. Spencer Campbell had an outstanding week of practice and would continue against the Tigers with 20 points. Butch Wininger would follow with 11 as he was the only other Cardinal in double figures. I played a few minutes at guard and finished with only 3 points with the only field goal being a lucky bounce. The headlines said. "Tigers Edge Cards" but we had lost 65-58. Crap, we're now 2-5. Are we headed for the bottom again?

The next game we went back to our normal starting line up and bested Daleville 71-59. You may recall we had lost to them earlier 68-64. In a well balanced offensive attack Jerry Mifflin lead us with 14, Butch Wininger garnered 12 and Phil Glaze chipped with 11, Spencer Campbell and I had 8, Tom Robbins and Bob Colter had 6, Bill Long had 4 and Bruce Carpenter had a basket. Well balanced. We are now 3-5.

DeSoto came over to visit us in our next encounter. They were 5-5 and wouldn't be taken lightly. As it turned out it wasn't even close as we prevailed by an astonishing score of 63-21. I was fortunate enough to lead the attack with 15 points while Bob Colter had 10 in another well balanced attack. We were now 4-5 and faced Selma on their home floor the next night. We are now 4-5 but that's not respectable considering what we had anticipated.

At Selma the next night we had a cat fight. We had trailed at all stopping points prior to the end of the game. We won 57-53 and I recall a couple of key rebounds bouncing my way at the end. Tom Robbins led us with 20 points, I chipped in with 11 and good old reliable Bob Colter had 10. We were finally back at .500 but still well below our expectations.

Next was the county tournament. We would open against DeSoto with Royerton and Center in our bracket. We had just had the better of the Panthers 63-21 so we felt pretty good about our first round draw. However, DeSoto would have nothing of a repeat and chased us all the way to half time. We were lucky to lead by 27-23. They had already scored more at the half then they were able to do only a few days earlier in a full game. We pulled out to an 11 point lead 37-26 by the end of the third quarter. The Panthers then went to a full court press, something Coach Boggs had prepared us for, so the write up went like this, "DeSoto threw a full court press at Bob Boggs' varsitymen in the fourth stanza in a desperate bid to get back in the game. However, the Cardinals refused to rattle. Looking for only the good shots, they hit on seven of nineteen and outscored the Panthers 16-9. In a continuing well balanced attack, Phil Glaze was the only Cardinal in double figures with 14 points." Well, we are now finally above .500 at 6-5. We would face the Royerton Redbirds next to whom we had lost earlier 54-50.

In our semifinal game with the Redbirds we would again have a nip-and-tuck encounter with them. The Muncie sports pages went like this.

"Royerton and Harrison met in the night cap, a game regarded by many observers beforehand as a tossup. As it turned out, it was a nip-and-tuck affair for three periods before a 'hot' fourth quarter enabled the Redbirds to carry off a well-deserved 59-53 triumph." So we had lost and were now only 6-6.

"The game was close with Royerton leading nine times, the Cards led six times and the score had been deadlocked ten times." No matter. The Redbirds would be runners up to champion Gaston. We had outscored them by three field goals but lost at the charity stripe. I had scored 12 and Jerry Mifflin 11 in this loss. No one else got to doubles.

Following the county tourney, we would face the champions, the Gaston Bulldogs on their home floor. After leading by eight mid way in the third quarter, we would succumb by two, 56-54. We had given it a go on their home court. But again, no matter. Butch Wininger would lead us with 19, and Phil Glaze would kick in 14. We were now an undesirable 6-7 and the Bulldogs remained undefeated at 14-0.

Junior Varsity Takes Second County Championship

These notes would be completely inadequate without mentioning that our reserves took their second county tourney in a row. I had not played with these guys since our undefeated and champion eighth grade team. Of course, I wanted to be with the varsity but in retrospect I did miss out on these sweet victories.

The lineup had Mark Pitzer, our submarine throwing baseball pitcher and John Ramsey, who was playing his first year of high school basketball, at forwards, the tall and crafty southpaw John Murphy at center, and Bob Murphy, John's older brother, and Larry Bailey at guards. They would avenge their only earlier loss by beating Royerton in the final game, 48-36. Their record stood at 17-1 following this encounter. That's quite a bit better than the varsity's record.

The varsity was next paid a visit by Mooreland from neighboring Henry County. You may recall that the previous year the infamous Harry

Shelby had presided over a whistle calling episode against us Cards and the Bobcats had prevailed by netting 33 free throws. This one would be different. We would prevail in a defensive struggle 41-33. I chipped in with 13 while Butch Wininger led us with 14 points. We were now back at 7-7.

A couple of nights later we entertained Ridgeville, a visitor from Randolph County. We scored well and came away with a 71-50 victory. I had 17 points, Butch Wininger had 16, Spencer Campbell broke out with 13 and reliable Phil Glaze chipped in with 12. We are now above .500 at 8-7. Things were looking up we thought.

As we traveled to Cowan and their wooden backboards, we were feeling like we might be getting there. Alas, it was not to be as we played the worst game of the season and lost 65-45. I countered with 12 points, the only Cardinal to break into double figures. We were really down and back at 8-8 or .500.

It was about this juncture when Coach Boggs decided that we needed to focus on defense since we usually could do some scoring. Not counting our last encounter with Cowan, of course. We painstakingly were introduced to the 1-2-2 zone defense and were patiently walked through our movements as we were led by Coach. Always with a point man, and always moving as a unit, we moved from side to side and then back again. Eventually we started to get it.

Also, it was at this juncture when Coach started us on an up scaled conditioning program which I mentioned earlier and the Saturday practices. Across one end of the gym to the theater seats, up to the top and across the top row of the seats, down the other end, across the other end of the floor to the side stage area jumping to reach it, across the stage and out the other side stage onto the floor. It was an excellent conditioning drill and we ran hundreds of laps over the next few weeks. In total honesty, I have never been in that kind of shape in my entire life, both before and after those drills.

Our next encounter would be against the panthers from DeSoto over at their goal house. We would bounce them 75-51 with Phil Glaze scoring

23 counters, Butch Wininger and I 15 each and Spencer Campbell 13. We lead substantially at every stopping point. We were now over .500 at 9-8 and running our tails off in practice while focusing on the 1-2-2 zone defense.

Next, we went over to face the Albany Wildcats on their home court. We were now above .500 for the second time all season. We would win this one 57-39. Geez, that zone is starting to work. I was lucky and garnered 15 points to lead the Cards while Butch Wininger tossed in 14 for the only other double figure we could manage. I recall working all day that day, a Saturday, and had been on my feet all day but needed some jingle in my pockets I thought, and felt tired from the beginning. We were now at 10-8 and things were looking up after our devastating start.

In our next to last scheduled game was against Center, a game we would win by a tally of 69-43. That zone's working pretty well by this juncture. Phil Glaze and Butch Wininger both tossed in 17 points, Jerry Mifflin had 12 and I followed with eight in a well balanced offense. Things are now rolling and we are 11-8. Conditioning is working and so is the zone.

Our last scheduled encounter would be against Stoney Creek a very small school so we were confident we would prevail. We did by a score of 87-34. Coach Boggs, in an effort to keep things reasonable put 13 Cardinals into the fray with all 13 scoring at least one field goal. We had finished with a flourish, winning six of our last seven games and settled at 12-8 for the season.

Our slow start would dampen the season, however, but with our zone not in the picture we had lost four of those early games by a total of only 12 points. There were two-2 pointers and two-4 pointers. Put those on the left side of the ledger and it could very well have been a 16-4 record. While this is total conjecture, it is more representative of the broad talent that this squad possessed.

Convinced we could do more we now prepared for the Muncie sectional tournament. As teams prepared we were still running and practicing the zone.

Seasonal records were as follows:

1. Gaston, 19-2
2. Eaton, 15-5
3. Cowan, 13-7
4. Yorktown, 12-7
5. Harrison, 12-8
6. Center, 10-9
7. Royerton, 10-12
8. Selma, 8-11
9. DeSota, 7-12
10. Daleville, 6-13
11. Albany, 3-17

So after all the prognostications before the season this is where we lined up for sectional play. While we had progressed to the upper echelon, we were not where we should have been. Our scoring for the season always listed Phil Glaze some where near 10th in the county, Butch Wininger always near 15th and me always around 20th. A better percentage on my free tosses surely would have garnered another 10-15 spots upward. But our strength was balance and now we were in shape and had that 1-2-2 zone defense.

Our first sectional encounter was against Yorktown, a team that had beaten us rather handily earlier in the season at their goal house and while Coach Boggs was still doing some experimenting. Our thoughts were mostly ambivalent as we got ready for this encounter. We knew we could do it and do it we did with that zone defense.

I recall the first quarter being almost scoreless as Yorktown, unable to figure the zone out just stood and held the ball for several minutes. No shot clock. The quarter ended 3-2 in favor of the Tigers. Not a single field goal was notched during this first period. They had finished one notch above us in the seasonal standings as you may recall from above.

We bounced the Tigers 56-37. There's that zone defense again. We all were yanked for the bench in the fourth quarter when the lead grew to 21 points. We again were somewhat balanced in our scoring with Phil Glaze netting 17, Butch Wininger 14, Jerry Mifflin 12 and I followed with nine counters. Do you have your abacas handy, that's now a record of 13-8.

We faced the DeSoto Panthers again and they were again fired up. After three losses to us this year, you would have been too. We had lost three to champion Gaston a year earlier but then bombed them in the sectional 57-44. Although we trailed at the end of the first quarter, 14-13, we would not trail at any other stopping point. Using what seemed like a plethora of reserves, the local paper said we simply wore them down in the later stages of the game. Remember the conditioning drills? Nine of ten Cardinals would score with Phil Glaze leading the way with 14, Jerry Mifflin followed with 12, and I came next with 9. One writer put it this way, in paying me, what was probably an unearned compliment, "Although he was not one of the scorers, Ralph Wray was an effective operator for Harrison. The big forward got all of his points in the first quarter, when they were needed to pacify a DeSoto team that appeared determined to fashion the second upset of the Friday-afternoon session."

The only on the court injury that I recall encountering was an elbow, or elbows from two big Panthers. Bill Nicely, who had left Harrison after our eighth grade championship year, and Bob Marks. As I maneuvered toward the basket they suddenly collapsed on me and started grabbing anything they could to get the ball. It was almost like being in a boxing match with two larger opponents. They whammed me directly in the nose. Not too much blood but I couldn't see and my eyes watered profusely. After a foul was called and an emergency time out, along with a minute or two, I was ready to carry on and did so. Are you still counting? We now are 14-8 and heading into the sectional semifinals. Not too bad for a 1-4 or 2-5 start. We are now 12-3 since that 2-5 start. We are still running and DeSoto is the only team to break 50 points against our 1-2-2 zone.

On Saturday afternoon of the 1957 sectional finals we would face Selma. We had bested them by 4 points before our conditioning work and newly discovered zone defense. Selma had beaten Muncie Burris in their last sectional encounter. This was the upset referred to above. We would break this one open in the last quarter to win 57-38. The score was tied 10-10 at the end of one. We Cards led at halftime, 22-19 and after three quarters, 38-32. Again we were balanced in scoring with sterling Phil Glaze popping in 16, I would follow with 12 markers and Jerry Mifflin getting 10. Two things. You've heard them repeatedly before. Our zone defense held the Bluebirds to only 38 points and we pulled away after they tired and we didn't. We are now 15-8.

Writer Jimmie Jones, in tourney Sidelights column, would say, among other things, "Harrison's 57-38 victory over Selma marked the first time the Cardinals have advanced to the sectional final since Coach Bob Boggs began guiding the team five years ago."

"Boggs cited excellent teamwork of his squad and good rebounding as the big reasons Harrison won the semifinal opener. 'We moved the ball around and worked together on defense,' he said."

"He praised Ralph Wray, Jerry Mifflin and Bob Colter for their outstanding rebounding performance, and Phil Glaze, aided by Wray and Mifflin, for pacing the scoring. The three accounted for 38 of the total points."

Are you still counting? On to the Bearcats of Muncie Central who had finished their regular season 15-5.

The pre-firing news articles indicated that the two Muncie schools, Central and Burris were, in all probability, headed for the first sectional final meeting in several years. Muncie Central, playing on their home floor, of course, was the favorite after a 15-5 season. And, they had stolen one of our best, Dean Campbell, who played regularly for them. Specifically, the newspaper said, "Burris, although only 8-11 in all games, has been better than a .500 ball club since the first of the year and is capable of giving the 'Cats a stiff argument." I knew some of the Owls including Rich Porter, whom I played some junior baseball with and

Rich had spent his eighth grade year at Harrison before returning to Burris. Knowing them and their capabilities, we weren't impressed. And we were right. If Selma could take them out it proved our point. Nothing, of course, was said about our Cardinal record of 6-1 since the third week of January.

I had played with and against some of the Bearcats over the years including the Sertoma baseball champions with Dave Holfheinz, Dean Campbell, our two letterman, who left for his senior year to join the Bearcats and Larry Wilkerson whom we had bested along with his Blaine team mates as eighth graders. And we had met other Bearcats on a casual basis. So we knew them pretty well.

The Muncie Star story went like this. "Muncie Central steam-rolled a game Harrison team Saturday at the Fieldhouse to win its 10th straight sectional basketball championship." Any questions about the home court? The story continues like this, "Final score was 68-44. They led Coach Bob Boggs' Cardinals at the quarter 20-12, at the half 35-24, and at the close of the third, 53-31."

"Firing without hesitation over the Harrison defense, the Purpleclads thrust eight field goals in 16 attempts for an even .500 in the first quarter and 13 of 30 through the first half for a big .433." Uh-Oh, they've solved our zone by just popping it in from long range. "Harrison was held to 55 shots by the aggressive Central defense and hit on 13 of them for .236. The losers got 18 points in fouls, Central 12." Those statistics are telling in that we were accustomed to hitting the basket for a much higher percentage while holding opponents to somewhere in the range as we were able to deliver in this contest. The Bearcats were very tenacious on defense. It was the real story of this one. My most pleasant remembrance was out jumping Larry Wilkerson for an offensive rebound and flashing an over the head reverse lay up past him. As players, we never noticed very much the crowd's reaction although on this one I heard it clearly and I thought the house was coming down. Not as good as a win but I had to settle for it. So, we are finished for the year at 15-9. We were 9-2 after our up-scaled conditioning program and 1-2-2 zone was installed. In our first eight games of the season we allowed an average of 64 points per game, and, excluding the final encounter with Muncie Central, in our last seven games we reduced this to a mere 42. Need we say more about that 1-2-2 zone. Central's tall center, Ted Sterrett, had been held to two field baskets.

Phil Glaze would notch 10 points, all on free tosses and I would garner three field goals. Butch Wininger would net eight and Bob Colter another 6.

Phil Glaze would finish the tournament third highest in scoring, with 57 points, immediately following the tall Muncie Central center, Ted Sterrett, who stood 6-8 and whom we held to two field goals in our encounter. I would finish down the ladder a bit in eighth place with 36 points, Jerry Mifflin in 10th place with 34 points and Butch Wininger in 13th place with 29 points. In selecting all tournament births, the sports writers had Phil on the first five players, myself topping the second five, with honorable mention going to Jerry Mifflin and Butch Wininger.

A great second half of the season but unmentionable first half. Here is where everyone stood following the sectional win of Muncie Central.

	Wins	Losses	Pct.
Gaston	21	3	.875
Muncie Central	19	5	.792
Eaton	17	6	.739
Harrison	15	9	.625
Cowan	13	8	.619
Yorktown	12	8	.600
Center	11	9	.550
Royerton	11	13	.458
Selma	9	12	.429
MuncieBurris	8	13	.381
DeSoto	7	13	.350
Daleville	6	14	.300
Albany	3	18	.143

Cards in Action 1956-57

Long Bill Long rebounds, Jerry Mifflin on left, Ralph Wray in background

Harrison's Ralph Wray (55), center, DeSoto's Bill Niceley, left and Bob Marks, right.

Looks like Ralph Wray doesn't like the zebra's call with Jerry Mifflin (43) and Spencer Campbell (45)

Ralph Wray grabs a rebound and looks for the outlet pass

Photographs furnished courtesy of the Star Press

Junior Class Cardinals, 1956-57

Spencer Campbell

Tom Robbins

Dennis Stanberry

Bruce Carpenter

Bill Long

Ralph Wray

Cards in Action 1956-57

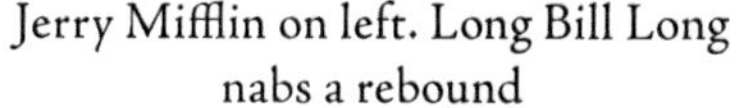

Jerry Mifflin on left. Long Bill Long nabs a rebound

Jerry Mifflin in action

1956-57 12 Victories, 8 Defeats

Front Row L to R: Student Managers Dick Cline and Wayne Nee Middle Row L to R: Bob Colter, Bill Long, Jerry Mifflin, Ralph Wray, Bob Murphy and John Murphy. Back Row L to R: James Wininger, Phill Glaze, Spencer Campbell, Coach Bob Boggs, Larry Bailey, Tom Robbins and Bruce Carpenter

Photographs furnished courtesy of the Star Press

Runnersup in Muncie Secional

1957 Muncie Sectional

Front Row L to R: Dick Cline, student manager: Phil Glaze, Butch Wininger, Tom Robbins and Bruce Carpenter. Second Row L to R: Ralph Wray, John Murphy, Jeff Mifflin and Bob Murphy. Third Row L to R: Hal Platt, assistant coach; Lowell Cline, Principal; Coach Bob Boggs, Bill Long, Wayne Lee, student manager and Bob Colter

Photograph furnished courtesy of the Star Press

On to our senior year.

Senior

As we approached our senior year of basketball we could hardly wait to get started. After all, we had an undefeated and championship eighth grade year, and two reserve team county championships under our belt although being bumped to the varsity as a freshman and sophomore had not allowed me to personally experience the euphoria of these reserve championships. It was our year! And, we had played our eighth grade year without sharp shooting and heady guard Tom Robbins. Why shouldn't we feel good about our chances?

The roster as it appeared in the local press for our 1957-58 season was as follows:

1. *Tom Robbins, G, 5-8 ½ , 143, Sr.
2. *Bill Long, F,C, 6-3, 155, Sr.
3. John Ramsey, F,C, 6-2, 202, Sr.
4. *Bob Murphy, F,C, 6-3, 149, Sr.
5. *Ralph Wray, F,C,G, 6-1, 176, Sr.
6. Mark Pitzer, F,C, 6-2 ½, 162, Sr.
7. *Bruce Carpenter, G, 5-8, 150, Sr.
8. *Spencer Campbell, F,C, 6-1, 154, Sr.
9. Dennis Stansberry, G, 5-9, 147, Sr.
10. Wayne Clements, G, 5-6, 126, Sr.
11. John Murphy, C, 6-4, 165, Jr.
12. Larry Bailey, G, 5-11, 132, Jr.
13. Jeff Clements, G, 5-6, 129 Jr.
14. Clement Spence, F,G, 5-7 ½, 160, Jr.
15. Don Addison, G, 5-6, 140, Jr.

*Lettermen

So there's the top fifteen. All but Jeff Clements, Clement Spence and Don Addison would be limited exclusively to varsity action while these three would get valuable development time in reserve action.

The Muncie newspapers would introduce the Cardinals by saying "Prospects Bright for Top-Flight Harrison Quintet Despite Loss of Four '56 Starters." We had our last two seasonal introductions being slightly overstated. Was this to be a repeat? The answer was a resounding NO!

Writer Jimmie Jones would put it this way. "Although only one starter is back from the squad that drove to the sectional finals before losing a 68-44 decision to Muncie Central last season, Harrison Township's Cardinals have prospects of becoming one of the county's top outfits this season."

"Coach Hal Platt steps into the head coaching position after being assistant to Bob Boggs the last two years. Boggs is now the Selma cage pilot."

"Ralph Wray, a 6-1, 176 pound senior, is the only starter in the six lettermen back for duty. Wray was a key figure in the Card's drive to the sectional finals last year. Wray earned a second team berth on the Star's All-Sectional squad. Other vets are Tom Robbins (5-8 ½), Bill Long (6-3), Bob Murphy (6-3), Bruce Carpenter (5-8) and Spencer Campbell (6-1)."

"Other seniors on the squad are John Ramsey (6-2), Mark Pitzer (6-2 ½), Dennis Stansberry (5-9) and Wayne Clements (5-6). Five juniors are up from an outstanding reserve outfit that finished with a 21-1 record and won the county reserve tourney last season. Included in the group are John Murphy (6-4), Larry Bailey (5-11), Jeff Clements (5-6), Clement Spence (5-7 ½) and Don Addison (5-6)."

"With plenty of height and promising juniors, the Cards should kick up a lot of trouble for their opponents this season."

"The Harrison club is noted for being a slow-starting outfit and Platt hopes to avoid early season setbacks. 'We will try for a good start', he said. He pointed out that the team started slowly last year but finished strong."

Are we going to be forever jinxed?

We would start at Eaton. They had the better of us the previous year in overtime 60-58. As I was getting accustomed to a new role of setting up our three big guys, I realized this would be a different year with a different role to play. Get those assists and let's win. After a total of 64 personal fouls were whistled we found that I, along with Tom Robbins and Bruce Carpenter were banished from the fray for 5 infractions. I recall Coach Platt laughingly saying to me just after my last personal, "Well, at least you got yourself another basket." I had reentered the game only seconds before and knocked down a fast break pull up from the circle.

Although I had played a little guard earlier in my career, I had not done so in about three years. This year it was exclusively at the guard position. I would quickly learn how to feed the three big guys who positioned themselves in a double post and significantly closer to the basket than Tom and I from our guard positions..

We led at all stops, 16-14, 37-23 and at the end of three quarters 51-38, and at the end 73 to 55.. Bill Long, while not a starter in this our first game (he would start every one of all the following games), led us with 19 points. Bill would go on to be our leading scorer. Big Moose Ramsey followed with 14 and John Murphy would chip in with 11. Tom Robbins and I had eight apiece having left early on personals. So our big front line had done its job and Tom and I played our role as guards. So, we are now 1-0, better than last year at 0-1.

Our second game would have Center's Spartans visit us for our first home game. Center had outstanding Mike Readnour who would later play for the Ball state Cardinals. Cowan had bested the Spartans in the first game 55-53. We weren't challenged and would prevail 78-51. Bill Long would lead us again with 18 points, Tom Robbins had 16 and John Murphy netted 14. I had eight and our other starter, John Ramsey had five. We're now 2-0 and off to a better start than last year.

Daleville's Bronchos paid us a visit in our third encounter of this our senior year. As the local paper said, "Undefeated Harrison made it three in a row with a lopsided victory over Daleville at Harrison." Once again, long Bill Long led us with 23 points, I chipped in with 17, Moose Ramsey had 15 and reserve Mark Pitzer had 10. Gee, we're now 3-0. What can I say?

Next was Royerton and their reputation of winning. But we had them at our goal house. The local news reporting put it this way, "Coach Hal Platt's undefeated Cardinals took their toughest opponent of the season in stride and captured a 90-70 victory over Royerton's Redbirds at Harrison."

As it turned out, our guys had bombed in field goals at a .405 clip. Not bad for high schoolers at that time. We were lead by long Bill Long and John Murphy both with 22 points, Moose Ramsey with 17, reserve Larry Bailey with 15 and Tom Robbins with 13.

I scored but a single point, having picked up a third personal foul midway through the first quarter, as I slid over to cover their outstanding forward, Norm Locke, before our big guys could get back on defense. Oops, that head fake got me. No matter, with reserve Larry Bailey doing a journeyman's job, I caught some unaccustomed splinters the rest of the game. But we were now 4-0, a good improvement over year earlier when we were 1-3 at this time.

Then we went over to Gaston, who had won the last two county championships, but were now without their playmakers, lost via graduation. We led at half-time 42-24 and would go on to win 72-48. Once again long Bill Long would lead us with 25 markers and John Murphy would throw in 17. That was all we needed as none of the rest of us could get into double figures. I do recall an easy fast break basket that only required a full speed head fake to freeze the Gaston defender. One Gaston patron would later volunteer to me, "while you didn't score with the leaders, you were one of the very best players out there." What's happening, we are now 5-0, and tied with DeSoto for the county percentage lead.

Both DeSota and us Cardinals would win our next encounters to stay tied at the top of the round ball hierarchy We would best Cowan in our closest encounter to date. DeSoto had earlier won their sixth battle. Against Cowan, we were led by our outstanding reserve Larry Bailey with 17 counters, long Bill Long and John Murphy would pitch in 15, Tom Robbins had 12, Moose Ramsey had 11 and I, bringing up the rear had nine. We are now at 6-0.

Then Yorktown came for a visit. Before the game got rolling, Yorktown Coach Earl Snider, would have us switch baskets from the ones on which we had warmed up. I suppose it was to try to throw us off and he clearly had the option. This was the only time in some 100+ games I was involved in that his happened. But it didn't work and failed to slow us down a single step. Normally, I would line up in the back defensive position at the opponents free throw line, but this time, probably because of the last second change of goals, I lined up on the side away from the circle and whispered to Moose Ramsey that I would be breaking down the side should he get the tip. He did and he finger-tipped it over to me as I went hell bent toward our goal. After a couple of stutter steps and even a couple of changes of pace, I pulled up on the Yorktown defender for an eight-footer. Bingo! We are off and running less than ten seconds into this one. Coach Snider's attempt to through us off hadn't worked. We would win this one 85-60.

We are now alone at the top of the percentage race since DeSoto had now lost a couple. John Murphy would lead us with 17 points, I chipped in with 16, long Bill Long and Moose Ramsey both had 15 and our sharp guard Tom Robbins had 10. We are now 7-0. Wow!

Herb Silverberg, in his column, Watching the Fouls, had this to say. "Harrison Township, with a team composed of reserves of the 1957 sectional runners-up and only a single starter under 6-0, is probably the most powerful contender at present." Well Herb was not accurate on all counts since I had started the prior two years and the prior three years if you choose to count my freshman year as a part-time starter.

Oh well, I was reminded of an article some years after we all had graduated when a local writer was naming all the Cards in a column and talked about the two reserve championships and our two sectional runs and seasonal championship. I was not mentioned. I was asked about this directly by a fan and all I could say was that I never played on those reserve champion teams since I had been bumped upstairs to the varsity. Sometimes a little research is good especially when you are using names. I know that well since I would later work in daily newspapers for over 20 years, albeit on the management side. At any rate, we are getting the press coverage.

In our last encounter prior to the Christmas and New Year's Holidays, we laced Daleville 73-36. That made it 8-0 and we all had excellent holidays. In the Daleville encounter we were led by big southpaw John Murphy who netted 20, followed by Moose Ramsey with 15 and long Bill Long would get another 11. It's Christmas and we are now 8-0.

After the holidays we went over for a visit to DeSoto who were 8-2 prior to the game.

We changed that as we had the best of them 64-51. John "Moose" Ramsey would lead the way, along with big John Murphy, with 16 counters, long Bill Long would get 13 and reliable Tom Robbins had 10. Guess what, we are now 9-0.

We would follow with a home game with Selma, coached by our previous Coach Bob Boggs. This turned out to be a total wipe out. We won 76-21. I had significant empathy for Coach Boggs since I knew that he had developed us Cards for five years previously. He also had gotten us into tip top shape the year before and had patiently taught us the art of the 1-2-2 zone defense. These were the two reasons we had made our surprising run at the end of the previous season. His coaching was behind both. I recall, after having stolen several attempted passes by the Selma guards into their forwards and center, that Coach Boggs was yelling at his guards that I was backing off. I was and was having an easy time of making the interceptions. Ten men scored for us as we starters played about one-half of the game, having led 38-15 at half time.

Long Bill Long had 15 markers, Moose Ramsey 11, Tom Robbins and I both had 10. Not too bad for half a game. Our math teacher and class sponsor, Maurice 'Mike' Kennedy, would stop me as we began warming up for the following Monday's practice, and volunteered that he thought I had played the most outstanding game for the Cards this year in our battle with Selma. I really appreciated that since I was still in my adjustment period as a guard. We now stand at 10-0.

Our last encounter prior to the county tournament was against Gaston at home. We would have little difficulty with the graduation depleted Bulldogs and prevailed, 79-56. In a well balanced attack, Moose Ramsey led us with 17 points, John Murphy had 14, long Bill Long and Tom Robbins had 10 and Larry Bailey and I would finish with 6. Well, we are now 11-0 and ready for the tournament something we had been waiting for since our eighth grade championship year.

The sports writers were cranking up and we were inundated with numerous press clippings although they all were not in sync with each other.

Jimmie Jones did a special article entitled "Harrison Cardinals 'Team to Beat' in County Meet." Well we must have believed it since we were not prepared as we had been in the previous year's sectional. We were not using the zone with our taller lineup and we certainly had not been pushed to get in top shape.

Jones's article, for the most part said, "Harrison Township's tall and talented Cardinals. Pacesetters of the county percentage race with a perfect 10-0 record (this was prior to our 11th victory over Gaston), will be the team to beat in the 30th annual county tourney, which runs Jan. 15 through 18 at the Muncie Fieldhouse."

"Coach Hal Platt's Cards are driving towards their first county title since 1931 and if the team continues its torrid pace the 1958 sectional could produce some big surprises."

"Last season Harrison, coached by Bob Boggs who is now the Selma mentor, went to the sectional finals before losing to the Bearcats. Four of the starters of that team are gone, but the remaining starters (sic), three of the season's reserves and a junior up from the outfit that had a

21-1 record and won the county reserve meet a year ago, have added up to a sensational winner."

"The Cards have a good bench to back up their starters, and Platt can always count in a capable replacement of one of the starters fouls out."

"The starting five consists of Bill Long, 6-3, John Ramsey, 6-2, John Murphy, 6-4, Tom Robbins, 5-8 ½, and Ralph Wray, 6-1, at guards. All of the starters except Murphy, a junior, are seniors. Wray is the only starter back from last season. "

"Capably backing up the starting five are Larry Bailey, 5-11 junior; Spencer Campbell, 6-1 senior; Bruce Carpenter, 5-8 senior; Mark Pitzer, 6-2 ½ senior; and Bob Murphy, 6-3 senior. The team has all around height."

"The Cards have assaulted the basket at a .393 percentage in the streak, caging 293 of 751 shooting attempts, with consistent hot firing. The team has a fine mark from the free throw line---sinking 195 of 306 for .637."

Here is where the starters stacked up as we prepared for an assault on our first county championship since the Yeager boys in 1931.

> Long Bill Long, .500 field goal average
> John Murphy, .382 field goal average
> Moose Ramsey, field goal average unknown at this time, .363 for the season
> Tom Robbins, field goal average unknown at this time, .376 for the season
> Ralph Wray, .443 field goal average

So, my role had shifted significantly from previous years, make those passes and get those assists (assists weren't recorded until later years). We were winning so this new role was working OK for me although several patrons frequently asked why "didn't you shoot instead of passing it off". Well it should have been self-evident, we had that tall timber closer to the basket. By the way, the flexibility required for this shift would arm me well for all the flexibility that is required in real life.

Coach Platt identified both Royerton and Eaton, who would win the 1959 county championship, as our toughest opponents.

Although there were a number of other newspaper articles which indicated that we Cards were the top heavy favorites for this year's trophy, it wasn't unanimous.

It would have been better for us to have had a few clippings for our locker room which indicated Royerton's Redbirds were favored. We only had Herb Silverberg's Watching the Fouls column, where buried beneath the column title, you find that he was picking Royerton. He even admitted that he had not seen us Cards in action so we discounted his dissenting opinion as irrelevant.

Surely the Redbird locker room was covered with things like this---"Harrison Cardinals 'Team to Beat' in County Meet" Or try this one as the tournament was ready to commence, "Undefeated Harrison Favored to Win County Tourney." Certainly we had the kiss of death written in these newspaper clippings but were too young and immature to realize it. Coach Platt where were you?

Coach Boggs, now the Selma mentor, passed along this one to me as we prepared for this writing. It was telling in an unusual way. It showed the connections of how many Johnny Hoosiers developed over the years. It is from the Muncie newspaper but is not a complete article, hence I'm not sure of the author although it very well could have been Silverberg. It was labeled simply, "And Still Royerton" and Coach Boggs had entered 1958 following the title.

In part, it went like this---"Two decades later, Center defeated Muncie Central in the sectional by a score of 29-27 score and the Spartan coach was also a former Royerton athlete, Morton Lambert, present county auditor and the younger brother of the George Lambert previously mentioned as the 'sixth man'."

"So, you get down to the present day and Royerton is once more a threat along with Harrison Township. Stauffer (Gordon Stauffer the Royerton mentor) looks back to his near upset of Central two years ago, 71-62, and is right about his 1957-58 array being far stronger than the team of that year."

"Well, what about Harrison Township? The Cardinals have been running wild at everybody's expense and piling up huge scores. How do I get a Royerton influence here? It's easy---most of the kids played with Boggs' club that went to the sectional finals last February. Yes, but wasn't Boggs a Selma star in his heyday? True---but all those Boggs boys got their early training at Royerton. Selma gained them just in time to win the county tourney three times in a row." Does any one doubt that the Boggs Brothers left a major imprint on our basketball history.

So, we had a bare locker room board to motivate us and Royerton's was full you can bet. And, Coach Platt was not one for motivational speeches. The only thing I recall from our locker room at the half of the Royerton game in the semifinals was to our student managers, my brother Donald 'Rudy' Wray and Dick Cline—"put those away, we don't need them" as he referred to the oranges and chocolate we toted along for halftime energy. Well, he did say one other thing, to me, get back in the game for Bailey. Larry had replaced me sometime in the first half but we had fallen farther behind.

We had beaten Eaton again in our opener, 67-42, having been led by long Bill Long and Tom Robbins with 15 counters apiece. We would next take out Daleville, 65-41, with Moose Ramsey netting 16 and long Bill Long getting 12 markers. Four of the rest of us would net 7-8 points in a balanced attack.

The headlines, on the day of the Royerton semi-final game would read, "County Tourney Favorites Clashing in semifinal." I don't suppose that, even at this late hour, we considered ourselves co-favorites. And, we were under prepared.

After we had lost to the Redbirds by a whopping 69-51 they would have a easy time with Yorktown in the final game to an undermanned Yorktown squad.

In the game with the Redbirds, they raced out to an eight point lead in the first period and led 37-19 at half time. The Redbirds were prepared and fired over .400 for the game. Wonder what a tenacious 1-2-2 defense could have done? As the last half started I knew we had a serious problem, something like 'Houston we have a Problem'. The truth of the matter is that we both scored 32 points in the last half. I recall racing up the floor with the ball in the last half following every Redbird goal, trying to get there before they set up their defensive alignment. The newspaper put it this way, "The Cards fought back in the third period as Wray scored eight points, but Royerton refused to fold and maintained its advantage." We finished on the losing side of a 69-51 score. Moose Ramsey would score 13 and I would add 10, all in the second half. No other Card would get into double figures.

Many would say if these two antagonists were to meet again in the sectional it would have burned the house down. I guarantee we would have been ready and motivated and have taken nothing for granted regardless of the newspapers. As fate would have it, we never met again. Moose Ramsey was selected on the all-tourney second team and the rest of us starters being named in the honorable mention column. Nothing short of seeing all five of us on the top ten would have been good enough, unless of course, we were champions. But then, there is a very high positive correlation between winning and being named on the select group.

Our old favorite, Herb Silverberg, summarized our demise rather clearly and accurately by saying, "this 1957-58 Royerton champion is probably one of the greatest of all-time title-holders---a club deserving to rank with such predecessors as Yorktown's Hensley-Mitchell-Beeman-Morrison-Reynolds array of 1955, the outfit which up to now has always stood out in the writer's memory."

"Coach Gordon Stauffer's classy combination was that impressive. And Harrison Township, despite its 18-point defeat at the hands of the new champions, is not one you should count out in this respect (in referring to the up coming sectional). The Cardinals, stuck on their 13th victory and unable to get off, were outgeneraled and outscored. But let nobody sell them short." So that's it, respect us but we're still not champions.

We are now 13-1 and without that county tourney trophy we had waited for since the eighth grade. Normally, this record would be considered outstanding but never was to us since we failed to reach that pinnacle of accomplishment. We had missed a golden opportunity.

Following the tournament, we would face Cowan at home. We prevailed once again 92-55. With our big three under the basket leading the way with Moose Ramsey's 19, long Bill Long's 13 and John Murphy's 12, we were never headed. Of course, seven other Cards scored from 5 to 9 points in an all out front to get off number 13. We did and are now 14-1.

We now had all five starters listed in the county's top 32 scorers. That's an abnormal ratio by any mathematician's count.

We would best DeSoto at home in our next encounter, 89-61. All five starters would score between 10 and fifteen points with Moose Ramsey again leading us with 15. We were really getting those assists on the left side down at this point. Moose and I both were left side players.

One remembrance is a little unusual. As the third quarter was coming to a close, with a couple of seconds on the clock, DeSoto scored. As Tom Robbins prepared to inbound to me I knew we were very short on time. With the clock running, Tom fired it to me and I took a couple of steps and let a two handed set shot go from about ten feet inside the out of bounds line at DeSoto's end. As I watched the flight of the ball I could see the shadow of the ball on the gymnasium ceiling, I thought if it gets there without hitting the ceiling it would be a miracle. It was as the ball fell cleanly into the basket. As we gathered for our huddle I still recall everyone laughing including Coach Platt. Not much was said as fans were in an uproar. That was my only two handed set shot that I can recall. Boy, I would trade that one for the county trophy. We are now a respectable 15-1.

We next traveled to Mooreland, where Harry Shelby had seen to it a year earlier that the Bobcats had 44 free throw chances, scoring 33 free throws. Well, no Harry this time but we were pressed and only won by 9 by a score of 54-45. Unbeknownst to us the Bobcats were a respectable 11-4 prior to our encounter. Long Bill Long had a magnificent game with 26 markers and Moose Ramsey had 13 to be second high. We are now 16-1.

As we headed into the final part of our season schedule, we now had six players, including reserve Larry Bailey, in the top 32 scorers in the county. That's darn near 20 percent. That's six of the 32 players in the county.

We faced the Albany Wildcats next. It was a runaway although the final score was only 74-57. We had lead at half 40-21. Moose Ramsey would lead the way with 19 markers, long Bill Long would get 17, I had 12 and John Murphy had 11. We are now an amazing 17-1.

We traveled to Center for our next to last game of the season. We led 46-28 at half time and were never in danger. We won going away 92-53. Moose Ramsey was now really getting the feel for things and scored 29 points, the highest for any Card in the entire year. Long Bill Long had 17, I had 15 and Larry Bailey, subbing for the injured Tom Robbins at guard had 12. We are now 19-1 with only Stoney Creek left. I hated that my four years of competition were coming to a close but, like all those before me, had no control over the marching calendar.

So we went over to Farmland to face small school Stoney Creek. We barely played much over a quarter of the game as all 12 players on the Cards team played and scored. That may be a record in itself. Reserve Spencer Campbell led us with 13 and long Bill Long had 10. It was an amazing scoring performance by all 12 Cardinals. We had finished at 20-1 but would have traded a few of those victories for one over the Redbirds in the county tourney.

Ok, the sectional is next. As it turned out we were bracketed with Gaston, Muncie Burris, Albany and the Center Spartans. All other strong teams, Muncie Central, Royerton and Eaton were in the opposite bracket. We were confident we would end up in the finals, unlike a year earlier when we did not have that confidence.

The sports writers had a ball in teasing the railbirds. In squad pictures published by the Muncie Star-Press, each squad was labeled with a cut line. The Cardinals line read "County Power---Harrison's Cardinals, regular season champs of Delaware County, face Gaston at 6 p.m., tonight in the opening game of the Muncie sectional tournament. Harrison goes into the sectional with a record of 20 wins and one loss." Gaston was simply labeled—"Tourney Underdog." They had won 3 and lost 16.

In his column, Sports Keyhole, Frank Levin, ventured to pick every game of this sectional. He would misfire on only one occasion, that being that he picked Cowan over Yorktown in the first round. The Tigers would nail this one by a score of 74-56. That would be his only miscue as he had this sectional scoped out with precision.

Herb Silverberg, despite not picking us Cardinals in the county tournament, had some positives to say about our group of guys. He started it this way, "From here, it looks like an extreme possibility that Royerton's Redbirds and the Harrison Township Cardinals may play in the finals of Delaware County's thirty-sixth annual sectional basketball tournament."

"There is a lot of talk about a semi final double feature next Saturday afternoon in which Burris would clash with Harrison Township's big Cardinals and the Bearcats would meet Gordon Stauffer's Royerton powerhouse." Well that's exactly how it played out. Herb continued, "Sometime ago, Royerton's athletic director, Harold Hutchison, was quoted in this corner as saying the Bearcats had better be 'up' when they played the Redbirds. And Stauffer himself has commented how much superior his boys are the team which almost surprised the Centrals two years ago. The score of that one was 71-62. So it isn't just a matter of opinion by this conductor."

"Incidentally, returning to something mentioned two paragraphs above, did you know that Hal Platt's Harrison's (sic) had gone over 90 points four times this winter, over 80 five times and over 70 on seven occasions."

So, let's go play.

Our first encounter was against the Bulldogs from Gaston, Our nemeses of the past two seasons. We got the best of the undermanned bulldogs, 62-43, having, led at all stops. Moose Ramsey would lead us with 21 markers and, our outstanding junior center, John Murphy, would add 14 markers. Six other Cards scored in another balance attack. That makes us 21-1. Yippee!

Muncie Central had little trouble with Eaton and Daleville took out Selma in other first round games.

We next had the better of Center's Spartans, 89-44. Although their outstanding center, Mike Readnour had 18, we were once again led by our tall timber. Moose Ramsey had 16, long Bill Long had 15 and center John Murphy added 13, and brother and reserve Bob Murphy had 10. I garnered nine with four other Cards in the scoring column. Are you moving that abacas? We are now 22-1. And, we face Muncie Burris in the semifinals with Muncie Central facing outstanding Royerton in the other bracket semifinal game.

As we warmed up for our battle with Burris, we were relaxed and confident. Although some writers had wavered on predicting the outcome of this one, ultimately, most agreed that we Cards had to be favored. We believed that also.

At the outset, the Burris defense was collapsing in front of our tall timber. No doubt their strategy was to bottle up our tall timber underneath. So, Tom and I started firing from long range. My first four shots fell cleanly through the nets and Tom was doing his part also. As Burris quickly started falling behind and called timeout, Moose said to me as we entered our huddle, "work it in" I was a little shocked but didn't respond. After all, we were pulling away and all the shots were falling. So, that's the only hint of dissension on this Cardinal team. We were a team and still have life long friendships.

We would get the best of the Owls, 70-48 with our reserves playing most of the last quarter. Frank Levin would say in his write up, "Coach Hal

Platt's Cardinals experienced much better fortune (referring to Royerton against Muncie Central when they lost 61-51) in the semifinals and led Burris all the way. Harrison took a 6-0 lead, and the Owls never came closer than four points. Harrison was ahead 21-14 at quarter, 41-25 at the intermission and 51-30 going into the final stanza."

"Coach Rex Rudicel's Owls could not cope with Harrison's height advantage and superior shooting."

"Harrison shot .462 in the first half and finished with.375 on 29 baskets of 77 tries. Burris averaged .260 on 19 baskets of 73 attempts."

"Long set the pace with 16 points, followed by Tom Robbins with 13 and Ralph Wray with 12. It was Robbins and Wray from their guard posts who got Burris hopelessly behind with their great out-shooting."

So we now face the Bearcats in the final game and are now 23-1. Not too bad for us country boys.

As the final game commenced, the Bearcats quickly scored. As I advanced the ball at the top of the key, the Bearcat defense laid back so I launched a twenty foot jumper which went cleanly through the basket. The Bearcats then quickly called for a timeout. We were barely into the fray. Later, it became obvious that Coach John Longfellow was berating their guards for not fronting us closely. He probably was thinking of the Burris game, earlier in the day, when Tom and I had a field day with the Owl's from Burris at the outset of that one. It worked, since the Bearcat guards would be a glove on our hand the rest of the way. Tom and I both finished with a single basket.

We trailed 15-10 at the first quarter mark, 33-20 at the half and 51-34 after three. We had managed to get the deficit down to five on three occasions in the third period. The Bearcats would call a couple of timeouts and then come right out and score again. Frank Levin opined as follows, "Muncie, which ran its record to 18 wins and six losses, was red hot against Harrison and shot .421 on 33 baskets of 76 attempts. In the first half, the Bearcats averaged .457." "Harrison regular season county champion, closed its campaign with a fine record of 23 wins and two defeats." But sophomore Ron Bonham had his way underneath and scored 14 field goals.

So, that's it. It is over. Was it a good year? Yes! But, we had closed out our high school years with out the county or sectional tournament trophies. We did manage a couple of sectional runners up experiences, a seasonal percentage championship, two reserve county tournament trophies, and an undefeated season and tourney championship as eighth graders.

Other than playing for the undefeated and tournament champion Olive Chapel Church following graduation and for a team made up of my high school mates in the summer basketball league played outside at the Saint Paul Methodist Church, located on 26th Street on Muncie's Southside, my basket trading career came to an end because of work, college and family. We were able to defeat the Ball State varsity team in this summer league and I was fortunate enough to be selected to the all star team, including several outstanding athletes from colleges and high schools including Muncie Central's Ron Bonham, at season's end.

Harrison Cardinals 1957-58

Front, Wayne Clements, First row (L to R) Ralph Wray, Bruce Carpenter, Larry Bailey, Tom Robbins, Dennis Stansberry, Manager D. Cline. Second row, Coach Hal Platt, Bob Murphy, John Ramsey, Bill Long, Mark Pitzer, John Murphy, Spencer Campbell, Manager Don "Rudy" Wray

Photograph furnished courtesy of the Star Press

Harrison Cardinals 1957-58 after the Muncie Burris Victory in Sectional
Kneeling front (L to R) Bruce Carpenter, Larry Bailey, Tom Robbins and Ralph Wray. Manager Dick Cline is seated next to Carpenter. Spencer Campbell and Mark Pitzer are kneeling behind front group.
Standing are: Principal Lowell Cline, Bob Murphy, John Ramsey, John Murphy, Bill Long, Coach Hal Platt and Don Wray, manager.

Photograph furnished courtesy of the Star Press

Cards in Action 1957-58

Bill Long (43) scores against Eaton, Mic Balle, Ben Hodgin, Don Love

(L) John Ramsey, Cardinals
(R) Rich Porter, Owls

John Murphy (45) Cardinal;
Rich Porter (34) Burris

John Murphy -1957-58

Photographs furnished courtesy of the Star Press

Cards in Action 1957-58

Long Bill Long and John Murphy battle for a rebound

Harrison's Bill Long (43), Ralph Wray (55). Eaton's Gary Clevenger (45)

Spencer Campbell nabs one for the Cards.

Photographs furnished courtesy of the Star Press

Cards in Action 1957-58

Mike Readnour of Center heads for the floor. Harrison John Murphy (45), John Ramsey (54), Ralph Wray (55). Harrison won 89-44

Harrison's Spencer Campbell (53). Royerton's Ron Pease (21), Jack Yoder at left and Ernie Slusher, right. Bob Murphy behind Yoder

Budge Hahn of Eaton dribbles low as Harrison's Tom Robbins (24) and Ralph Wray (in crouch) watch for mistakes. The Eaton cager in back of Hahn is Mic Balle.

Photographs furnished courtesy of the Star Press

1957-58

County Kids Cut Capers - Unbeaton Harrison
1957-58

Supporting Cast led by Carolyn Hargis

Photographs furnished courtesy of the Star Press

Bill Long
nabs a balloon

Chapter Fifteen

For the Record

In retrospect, while our disappointments were hard to swallow at the time, I think we were served well. We learned discipline, that nothing tops hard work, flexibility and that we should never believe our press clippings. This last Cardinal team of 1958 certainly has nothing to be ashamed of as adults. We produced two boys who have owned very successful small businesses, a scientist for NASA, an optometrist, a career military man who retired from the Pentagon, a college professor, a career businessman who was a senior officer in three separate and large corporations and with 14 years college teaching, an insurance executive and a multi-media specialist for a university.

For the record, other classmates accounted for themselves very well in the real world. Ten of the 1958 class at Harrison Township ended up with one or more college degrees. Seven of us budding adults ended up with a minimum of graduate degrees. Not bad for a class of gigantic proportions of some 28 youngsters. That's an amazing 36% and coming from a small school with limited resources. But we had the devoted and skilled teachers, although we gave them a bad time occasionally. Although I don't want to overlook anyone, and probably have, Barbara Heeter, Barbara Carter, Coach Bob Boggs, Mike Kennedy, Dorothy Nelson, Lowell Cline, Deva Adams, Cathy Fewell, John Wright and Eli Roscoe all come to mind. Mr. Penrod, who was our principal for several years, was an outstanding administrator, although his son Bruce, was an outstanding guard on that Royerton team that had the best of us as seniors in the county tourney. Then there were our elementary teachers including Bernice Oliver and Paul Metzger in the sixth grade. Thanks to all of you. We owe you a lot.

Well that's pretty good. Our early lessons both in defeats and in winning drove all of us to admirable heights in later life. And, that's what small school athletics or growing up in a value centered, effort required atmosphere can do for young people. As athletes, we also were fortunate to have been led by Bob Boggs and others like him. I wonder how these statistics stack up against other school athletes and other students?

As of this writing we have lost five of these life long friends from the Class of 1958. The first to leave us was Gary VanNatter, who was a good friend of mine but who grew up some decades before society had matured. Then there was Pat Hargis in an auto accident well before her time to go. And finally, we have lost Jim Ramsey, brother of Moose of basketball fame, Darrel Wray and last year, Lynda Byers.

Chapter Sixteen
High School Anecdotes

Although Gib was significantly worn down by all the details of what I had just related about our high school athletics, he was hanging in there. "Gib", I said, "here are some anecdotes from other Johnny Hoosiers while we were in high school. I enjoy just thinking about them and I am sure they will prove interesting to you". Gib was beside himself and wanted to hear them even if I chose to embellish them a little.

Bob Murphy

Bob Murphy, probably my closest friend in high school, relates three of his experiences that occurred when he and I weren't together. He first relates a story that datelines just after he turned sixteen. His father sat him and his brother John down at the dining room table for a discussion. I am confident that this came from Bob's father just being a good parent and not from anything these two had done since they were pretty much model kids. Both boys would play with us on our basketball teams throughout high school. In 1958 Bob was a 6'3' reserve and John was our starting center at 6'5'. Bob could out dribble most everyone on the team and John possessed the best left handed push shot in the county.

Bob's Dad said it would be short and sweet. And it was. Their father simply told both boys that "if you get yourself into trouble you will have to get yourself out of it." Of course they steered well clear of any distractive problems.

Lesson Learned: Follow the Guidance of Your Parents and Elders

Bob also tells of the night after basketball practice when he and three other friends thought they would challenge one local orchard owner who was overly protective of his orchard's bounty. Two of the boys were dropped off at the orchard, while the other two drove away with a plan to return shortly and pick up the intruders with their apples. As the two bounty hunters stood by the side of the road with their prizes, a car came slowly by. It was a cold and cloudy autumn night and darkness was complete. The two jumped in the car only to discover they had jumped in a car with an elderly couple. Oops! They quickly asked the couple to let them out of the car and they hence made their escape.

Lesson Learned: Look Before You Leap

Another experience which has its genesis with Bob, relates to a time when he and some other teenagers were stacking hay bales and driving them on a hay wagon to the storage barn. One of the boys had just turned sixteen and had a brand new driver's license. The new and untested driver berated Bob to let him drive until Bob relented. This exuberant, but untested, driver proceeded to dump the hay bales off the wagon when he drove the wheels of the wagon into the ditch. Needless to say, the only damage was that the boys had to reload the wagon prior to taking it to the storage barn.

Lesson Learned: Do Not Relent to Pressure, Even from a Friend.

Bob, with his amazing memory for details, also recalls how we would stay after school while in elementary school on days when our varsity had scheduled games at home. We played basketball in the high school gym from 3:30 p.m. until we were chased out at about 6 p.m., as our administrators prepared for the games that evening. We would grab a bowl of chili or a sloppy joe in the school cafeteria which was open prior to home games.

Lesson Learned: Take Advantage of Opportunities

He also recalled when he and I went to Louisville, Kentucky, to pick up a copy of my birth certificate that I needed to hire in at Warner Gear the year after we graduated. It turned out to be a little more than we had counted on since all government offices we closed that day since it was President's Day. Well, we survived by pooling our money for a room at the local YMCA. Bob recalls us walking around downtown Louisville that night with very little in our pockets but in awe of this city. We made it safely through our nocturnal walk around and got that certificate the next day without fanfare.

Lesson Learned: Everyone Needs a Good Friend

Bob also reminded me of another event that occurred on our senior trip to Washington, DC. We ended up in two groups at the US Mint as we toured the facility. Cathy Fewell, Janet Nauman and I were separated from our larger group of Harrison graduates. It seems that our classmate, Darrel Wray, he's the one that was heavily involved in the English class "bird in the desk" episode, had brought along an ample supply of "cracker bombs". I'm not sure of the component make up of these entertainment devices even today, but know when thrown on the ground they sound like fire crackers, or even more daunting, the firing of a gun.

Well, in traversing the multiple stairwells, Darrell in his mischievous way, dropped a few from several floors above and directly down the open stairwells. You can guess the outcome, the other larger group of Harrison graduates was quickly surrounded by security personnel and herded into a large conference room. Fearing a gun in the facility that minted all our US currency, they were taking no chances. I can't tell you what transpired in that meeting but can say that it wasn't a short meeting. All Cathy, Janet and I could do was wait on the outcome. That was the last time that Harrison township graduates ever toured the US Mint according to Bob. It makes sense so Bob is probably right on target on this one.

Lesson Learned: Think About the Repercussions

Bob also told me about the time that our classmate Dennis Beedle found a way to get into the very large air ducts which were all overhead in the 1924 constructed Harrison school building. Well, you can guess what old "Beede" did. Yes, he crawled around and had himself an entertainment feast watching most all of the classes going on in the various classrooms.

Lesson Learned: I Simply Do Not Know, Your Call

Bob mentions the time that Jeff Clements threw a baseball in game warm ups and struck Tom Robbins squarely on the side of his nose. You guessed, Tom's nose was broken, and the first pitch was yet to come. I know that was simply a freak accident but we couldn't afford to lose sure handed Tom.

Lesson Learned: Accidents Happen so Anticipation is Helpful

Bob mentioned that we once went over to the upstairs loft area at Carpenter's Hardware Store in Commack and had our own basketball practice in the loft of the hardware store. It was owned and run by Herman Carpenter, father of our teammate Bruce Carpenter. It seems that we were in a flu epidemic quarantine so we couldn't have our normal practices. So we did it and didn't miss out on practice.

Lesson Learned: With Ingenuity, Most Things are Possible

One of the things that Ralph Wray is least proud of, there are others of course that will not be mentioned in this writing, was brought to his attention by Bob. As a fourteen year old Ralph came home from school one day to find everyone gone and brother John's car parked squarely in the driveway with the keys in the bedroom. Temptation was too much. Ralph got the keys and thought he would go over and see his friend Tom Robbins at his house. Ralph first noticed that the gas level was unusually low. With some luck, the supply of gasoline would have been depleted quickly. No such luck.

As Ralph watched the fuel level needle, he thought he would stop and pick up Bob Murphy for a threesome at Tom's House. Fortunately, Bob's mother refused permission for Bob to go with him. As it turned out Ralph rolled the car over on a gravel stacked road a few minutes later and recalled all the flying dust and debris in so doing. He had hung on the steering wheel and came out unscratched. But, with Bob in the passenger side seat it might have been different. No seat belts back then. He thanks the powers to be that Bob didn't go with him. Ralph never mustered up the courage to apologize to brother John, who was away at a track meet at the time, So here it is---John I apologize and am very sorry. Your younger brother, Ralph. Ralph says, "if you need that one replaced, he can do it today."

Lesson Learned: Never Delay an Apology, and Secondly, Wait Until you are Old Enough

Bob would finally mention that Spencer Campbell would pick a Hurricane Six Willis over a 1957 Chevy as his father prepared to buy him his first car. The little Hurricane Six could run though. In a setup match against Mark Pitzer's Hudson Hornet, Tom Robbins would ride with Mark, and someone else, unnamed of course, would ride with Spencer to be sure everything was kept on the up and up. Just as the cars were firing off the starting point in this historic drag race, Tom, as planned, reached over and turned Mark's ignition off. It wasn't much of a match of course but Mark developed some unsavory vocabulary although it was short lived.

Lesson Learned: Stick to Your Choices, and secondly, Set the Ground Rules First

John Murphy

"Bob's younger brother and our star center on the basketball team, John, filled my ears with a few also. Here are some of them, Gib, for your enjoyment."

This one occurred the year after we had graduated and John was a senior himself. A young fellow by the name of Gene Goff was caught carving his initials into one of the pristine desks in our assembly room for the top four grades. Gene reportedly spent several free periods sanding his initials off the desk. It was as tough on the other students as it was on the young Mr. Goff because it sounded more like fingernails on a blackboard.

Lesson Learned: Respect Public Property

John also reminded me of the day we received our honor jackets for letters earned in our four years of athletics during an all school get together. This was traditional the week before the sectional tournament. I'm not sure if John recanted this or if he triggered my memory. I will, however give him credit. As Coach Platt pulled each honor jacket out and noted the chevrons on the right arm and stripes on the award letter, he pulled out one that had four chevrons for letters in basketball, four letters in track and four letters in baseball. It had to be Ralph Wray's since no one else had four years of varsity basketball. Ralph was astounded when Platt called Spencer Campbell's name. What? It must have been a Faith Hill precursor.

Ralph Wray would shortly receive his letterman jacket with four chevrons and four letters for baseball. But to make matters worse, only three letters for track. It seems that a lesson was to be learned for finishing everything you start since he had been docked for a track and field letter as a sophomore for skipping the county track meet. He had been told that Phil Glaze and he had been scratched from the county meet because of some girl thing. His Mother had told him, so you don't know to this day what source she had for that erroneous information. Ralph had earned the third highest number of points for the season but was still docked. Phil showed up and participated. The problem with Spencer's award was that he had been awarded letters for his freshman and sophomore years in both basketball and baseball that were earned by another Campbell—namely Dean Campbell. Spencer, within a week, had removed all his chevrons and letters to end the embarrassment every time he wore his honor jacket. No matter, Platt had been duped by the MENSA material Spencer.

Lesson Learned: Honesty First or You Will Pay the Price Later

John closed by mentioning an episode involving Tom Robbins and Spencer Campbell. It seems that Tom put some condoms in Spencer's jacket pocket. As Spencer was putting on the jacket in front of his Mother, Tom simply asked Spencer what he had in his pocket. Spencer, knowing nothing about the condoms, pulled them out right there in front of his Mom. No one can recall Spencer's explanation although anyone as bright as Spencer undoubtedly came up with something logical such as the condoms were for a tensile strength test in science lab.

Lesson Learned: Choose the Proper Forum

Jeff Clements

A life long friend of this writer, Jeff Clements, a year his junior, perhaps put it the best way of all in remembering our past and our growing up together in the 1950's. Jeff put it succinctly, "we're good friends, still after 50 years." And Jeff is one hundred percent correct.

Jeff recently rattled off some interesting anecdotes with which I was unfamiliar. He recanted the time he, and his one year older brother, Wayne, rode their bicycles down to the Murphy boys home just down the road a bit on Bethel Pike. As the Clements boys approached the driveway at the Murphy's they found that the Murphy's had deposited a large load of #8 pea gravel ready to be spread to enlarge their basketball area next to their garage. So they impetuously and quickly decided to ride full steam ahead and jump the somewhat large gravel pile. Not considering all the outcomes, they rode hell bent into the pile, only to be tossed head first over their handle bars with the bikes stopping at the front edge of the gravel. Fortunately, nothing was damaged except their budding and youthful pride.

Lesson Learned: Consider All Possible Outcomes

Jeff also mentioned a couple of other instances when they approached the edge of getting seriously hurt. Benny Benefield, about three years our junior, took a rock to the head which was intended for a mailbox. Another was a group of youngsters using walnuts for weapons in an all out war. Geez, we were lucky some times.

Lesson Learned: Same as Above, Consider the Outcomes

Then Jeff mentioned the time that the attractive young wife of Larry Bailey, whom Larry had met at Ball State University, tried her luck at cooking some rice. As the meal preparations began, Larry's wife, unaccustomed to these domestic duties started putting more and more rice into the holding pot and soon found that they had rice, rice and more rice, as the cooking process took place. It must have been a festive rice party.

Lesson Learned: You Can't be an Expert in all Fields

Jeff talked about the time that Spencer Campbell was riding atop a load of hay bales and when the hay wagon tipped over, no one could find Spencer. He was buried underneath all the spilled hay bales. But don't despair folks, Spencer arose again from the ashes. Phoenix.

Lesson Learned: We are Lucky Sometimes Even if We Do Not Consider the Outcomes

Then there was the case of the disappearing gasoline which cost an astonishing 19 cents per gallon. We won't say more about this one.

Lesson Learned: Inflation is Like Father Time, It Marches On

Jeff tells about the even handed discipline dealt out by coach Platt during his senior year after we 1958er's were gone. It seems that Jeff had been suspended for a game for some long forgotten reason. Shortly thereafter, star John Murphy, in his despair over a .500 season, chose to ride home from a game at Cowan with his parents and main squeeze, Sherry Sollars, rather than return on the team bus. This time coach Platt told the team he would leave the question of the suspension of John up to the team. They voted. Jeff says he was the only team member to vote for suspension. He was waiving his hands and almost jumping up and down when the votes were caste. Alas, stardom had its privileges, or was it that the players were sending a message with regard to Jeff's earlier suspension. Oh well. Both Jeff and John are still laughing about this one.

Lesson Learned: Leaders Must Apply Discipline Evenly

The final episode presented to me by Jeff, involved the night they were preparing for the annual fund raising carnival in the school gymnasium. It seems that one of the fellows had gained access to some beer, so several of the boys decided that it just couldn't go to waste and had a couple of pops apiece. They then went into the gym and went up to the top row of theater seats to be as far away as possible from school teachers and administrators. However, their conscience got the better of them as they thought Coach Platt surely was aware of their refreshments. So----they went down to "confront" him and did so. Nothing ever came of it though.

Lesson Learned: The Happy Hour Doesn't Fit All Occasions

John "Moose" Ramsey

Moose, to this day, is a friendly unassuming, self-effacing gentleman who has run his auto repair shop in Gaston for many years. He is a pure pleasure to be around. A fishing line and cold one is about all he and his adorable wife "Sparky" require for contentment. Moose enjoyed high school and is most proud of his rebounding trophy he earned as a senior star on the Cardinal basketball team. While Moose didn't play his first two years in high school, he played junior varsity as a junior and then became a bright and shining star for the Cardinals in his final year. He would have paid more attention to his studies if he had it to do all over again and says; 'I figured that two D's would get me through the final semester exam since two D's trump an F." Moose is very proud, and justifiably so, of his two offspring, one a minister and the other a school teacher.

Finally, Moose says he had fun with all his classmates, picking up corn and selling magazines to raise class funds for the growing treasury. He recants easily a story of several of us boys riding back from a track meet at Alexandria as seniors when Mark Pitzer came over an elevated railroad crossing at about 70 miles per hour only to have the infamous Hudson Hornet bottom out. Not just once, but twice. And, of course, there is the time when Joe Holmes, younger brother of our classmate Donald Holmes, brought his Dad's brand new Edsel and spun it around in front of the school. Yes, doughnuts were in way before NASCAR made them famous. Oh well, kids were kids and still are for that matter.

Lesson Learned: Youth Has Its Moments Without Good Judgment

Moose had an older brother Jim, also in the 1958 class. Unfortunately, Jim is one of the five class members who have now passed. But that's not my point here, it seems we had a repeat of the Yeager Brothers, Jim wouldn't go to school without Moose. So they started together when Moose became school age, just like Jim and Bill Yeager before them.

Lesson Learned: Brotherly Love is Strong

Phil Glaze

One of my lifelong friends, Phil Glaze, was an outstanding athlete even with his small stature. Pound for pound Phil was probably the best athlete around. Not only did he drive the family's John Deere tractor to baseball practice as a freshman, he was always on time. Phil, diminutive, but with excellent athletic skills, would later become a member of Delaware County's Athletic Hall of Fame for his prowess in softball after leaving high school. In high school he was a great pitcher and third baseman. He and Ralph Wray would rotate positions during Wray's junior year since both were limited to pitching nine innings per week. They would win the summer league championship before Wray had to lay out all but the final two games in the fall season because of a collapsed lung as a junior.

Lesson Learned: Determination and Perseverance and Ability leads to Success

Phil, a good looking and creative guy, grew tired of his tractor conveyance so he purchased his first car at age fifteen. That is something I would also do later. However, Phil had the market at the time on creativity. Since he couldn't get his driver's license until he was sixteen, Phil started to date a young lady that was sixteen years old since she had her driver's license. Well, at least that was one of the reasons for this dating duo. Phil would drive to his friend's house, which was out in the country, and then she would drive to town or wherever they wanted to go.

Lesson Learned: With a Little Ingenuity You Can Do Almost Anything.

Another thing that Phil reminded the writer of was how we looked forward to our celebrated senior class trip. Every graduating class used to take a weeks long trip to Washington DC and New York City. After traveling to both cities later on to transact business I fully understand now what a mind stretching event that must have been for a group of seventeen and eighteen year olds.

For instance, if you go to Manhattan Island in the heart of New York City, you can visit the Bank of New York and look across Wall Street at the New York Stock Exchange. Or, if you are a history buff, look the other way and see the historically significant church with its small and quaint graveyard in which notables are buried including Alexander Hamilton.

Phil, a hustler in most everything he does, notes that we used to go around to the local farmers during harvest season and go through their corn fields and pick up missed ears of corn that were missed by their corn picking equipment. We would take the corn to the local elevator for cash for our trip fund. We also used to have fund raisers such as skating parties and the annual fall school carnival. We always enjoyed them, not realizing at the time, how important the fund raising was since we were not financially endowed.

Lesson Learned: Work Hard and Save your Pennies

John Patrick Drayer

One of the phenomena's of high school back then was that most all boys and girls would pair off in what was know as going steady. I suppose this gave us social acceptance and ensured that we always had a date when needed. Anyway, Ralph Wray fell victim to that phenomenon during his first couple of years in high school to the chagrin of Coach Boggs. He was very protective of athletes since he had lost some earlier to pregnancies and much too early marriage. Things are very different today when you see high school stars even holding their offspring at athletic events. Coach was right, of course, as many of these early commitments end in disengagements. We were not mature enough to recognize what true love and commitment really are.

John Patrick Drayer was one of those that had it figured out even then, as he steadfastly refused to become involved in such a ruse. John thought this was silly and mostly for social status. He was right. In reality, we were all too young for that, and with some maturity, we would have all realized that. That is not to deny that some young loves last a lifetime. Brother John and his Phyllis, Jack and Hilda Sayre are exceptions to name two of those exceptions. Going steady was not, in most cases a function of love and commitment, but simply wanting to fit in socially.

If you were going steady, and had a class ring, your steady girl friend would wrap your ring with string of some sort and then apply nail polish to the string so it would fit her smaller finger. John Patrick, being wiser than most of us, would later say if you bought a ring you should wear it yourself. Of course, the writer fell victim to the social practice and seldom had his own class ring until he was in his junior and senior years. We received these mementos of our advancement toward graduation as sophomores.

Lesson Learned: Social Practices are not Always Good for You. Learn the Meaning of Commitment Before you Commit Yourself

Straight From the Writer

One of the things that rang true in the 1950's, and is still true in the minds and blood of young motor heads today, is drag racing and cars. Of course, some cars have been replaced by pick up trucks today. The writer calls his a "Tennessee Cadillac." The budding gear heads used to drag race wherever there was an empty road, usually at night so traffic would be minimized. Thank the Almighty for that insight. This was not an every week occurrence but occurred with some frequency. One of the writer's classmates, the submarine pitching southpaw, Mark Pitzer, owned a 1951 Hudson Hornet. It was a stick shift and would fly although the appearance was suspect. Mark never lost a drag race to my knowledge, except for the celebrated one where Tom Robbins turned off his ignition against Spencer Campbell's Willis. Mark's dad, a master motor mechanic, always kept it humming. The Hudson Hornet had some innovative engineering. For instance, the lug nuts were all in one piece with the lug and bolt being one piece. There was no female part to these lug nuts, that being part of the wheel hub. They haven't been made that way in years, to my knowledge, but that was an outstanding concept back then and seems to ring true even today. Since no one could beat Mark and his Hudson, we challenged him to see if he could drive that monster down the railroad tracks. He did it with very little problem by drastically reducing the air pressure in his tires allowing the Hornet to follow the railroad tracks precisely. I am glad, to this day, that few trains used the Gaston to Muncie railroad even then.

Lesson Learned: Some Things Do Not Change a Lot with Time

In our Junior English class, which met the first period following lunch, the episode of a "bird in the desk" occurred. One of my classmates, Darrel Wray, a mischievous chap prone to distractions, captured a sparrow and proceeded to put it into the top right hand drawer of the teacher's desk, where Cathy Fewell, our young attractive and new teacher, always kept her grade book. Mrs. Fewell always removed her grade book to call attendance at the beginning of every day. We knew this practice well. While absences were posted by the principal's office at the start of every school day, the first period following lunch required a second roll call since things sometimes changed at mid-day.

Well on this day, Darrel had his captured bounty and may have gone a little over the top when he put it in that top right hand drawer. As we waited for the inevitable, Darrel could hardly contain himself. When Mrs. Fewell finally opened that drawer after what seemed like a school day in itself, the sparrow flew out into the classroom frantically searching for a way out of the classroom. All hell broke loose, with Mrs. Fewell coming unglued and all the girls screaming. Darrel was almost rolling on the floor and then several boys joined in the chase of the poor sparrow. After about two to three minutes the poor sparrow was captured and released out the window. After verbally lashing us all we proceeded with class. I think we earned a pop quiz for this one.

Lesson Learned: Some Things Do Not Belong in the Classroom Including Sparrows

Another incident occurred in Mrs. Fewell's English class. This was a very immature and insensitive thing to do. Time will not change that. Since this class commenced immediately following the lunch break, we idiots had the opportunity to gather outside the door and wait for the bell to ring indicating that we should proceed to go in the classroom and take our seats. While Mrs. Fewell had already gone into the classroom and was ready to commence her lesson for the day, one of the group of boys that shall remain anonymous, had the idea that it would be funny for all the boys to enter the classroom one at a time and slam the door behind them each time. Well we did that. By the time we were all in the room, Mrs. Fewell was in tears. She left the room and returned with our Principal Lowell "toad" Cline. Well you can imagine the tongue lashing that we received. He had properly put us in our place. Incidentally, we had tagged him, affectionately, as the "toad' since he was always jumping on us. So it seemed.

Lesson Learned: Have More Respect for Authority and Don't Follow a Dumb Idea Even with Friends

Another door incident, mentioned by Ralph Wray, is recalled somewhat vividly. As he walked down the crossover hall to the men's restroom he would pass the music room in that hall way. As he did, the door came flying open, even somewhat violently, and struck his forehead right above his right eye, opening a one inch gash, that although shallow, blead profusely. As he ended up in the Principal's office for first aid, it became known that Donald Paul Ritchie, a classmate of Ralph's, was involved in some kind of horseplay in the unsupervised music room. Today Ralph carries a small reminder of this even into his seventh decade.

Lesson Learned: Accidents Happen Unexpectedly and in Places Which Seem Without Danger

When Ralph Wray was a sophomore, and his brother John a senior, Coach Walter Fisher of the Muncie Central football team, was the featured speaker at our annual athletic awards banquet. Their Dad had done some work for Walter when the Wray's lived on Godman Avenue many years previous. Father Wray was undoubtedly behind getting Walter to come out and speak to us. Walter was a real estate developer and farmer in addition to his teaching/coaching duties.

"If you want to improve your athletic performance at Harrison High," Walter said, "just go back down there and get some more Hoosiers (Wrays) in Kentucky. They used to practice as preschoolers by throwing rocks at my ducks on our pond."

He was right and we did it although never scoring any direct hits and never injuring any of those beautiful ducks. Little did the Wray's know at the time, but Bill Long, one of the stars of the 1958 basketball team hailed from Pall Mall, Tennessee, only about twenty miles from where John, Ralph and younger brother Donald 'Rudy' were all born in Southeastern, Kentucky. So Walter was right on target with his recruiting compass.

The other thing that Ralph recalls about this is that one of Harrison's young attractive females came up and said he should have seen his red face as Mr. Fisher was speaking about this. Well, all of us would grow up to treasure our ancestry even though there was some embarrassment about being one of those migrants from the hill country at this time in our young lives.

Lesson Learned: Be Proud of Your Heritage

"So Gib, tell me if you think these notes will have a positive impact on the younger generation? At least in terms of the lessons one must learn in order to become a contributing adult." Gib seemed introspective for a moment, always his thoughtful self.

Then he said simply, "only if they read this and are reflective." He then had a second thought. He said, "Johnny, we have had a couple of state champions, both girls and boys teams, here in Byrdstown with our beloved Pickett County Bobcats." I remarked that I was aware of that as we regularly go to the games where the girls start the process at 6:30 p.m. and the boys follow at 8 p.m. Being a much smaller school, the boys frequently play a few games against larger schools and normally win twenty or more games each season. One of the differences from the 1950's at Harrison Township is neither the boys nor girls put a junior varsity on the floor and, as a consequence, you frequently see freshmen and certainly sophomores playing regularly for the varsity. At any rate, there are some mighty talented young people out their representing us every game.

Even Dr. Larry Mason, our local head of the Byrdstown Medical Clinic, is avidly involved as team medical doctor and more so as high school golf coach. He's another jewel.

So, this writer hopes that this is enjoyed by all and that if a youngster takes a look at this it will assist them in growing to adulthood.

The Pre-School Years

The Elementary School Years

The Junior High School Years

The High School Years

Contributors List

1. Beedle, Jim, a great friend and high school mate, class of 1956
2. Bright, Jim, my father-in-law, with a great attitude
3. Boggs, Bob, a great coach and athlete
4. Boggs, Phil, a great athlete
5. Campbell, Judy (Yeager), a high school friend, daughter of Bill Yeager
6. Carter, Barbara, a great teacher and friend
7. Clements Jeff, a great friend and high school mate, class of 1959
8. Click, Garland, a great 92 year old and former school bus driver
9. Drayer, John Patrick, a great friend and former teammate, class of 1956
10. Glaze, Phil, a great friend and great athlete, member of the Delaware County Athletic Hall of Fame, class of 1957
11. Hayes, Taylor, a great coach and member of the William Penn (Iowa) College Hall of Fame
12. Heeter, Barbara, a great teacher who says she wants to be remembered as "a former teacher who hopes she has touched many students in a positive way".
13. Long, Bill, a great friend and teammate and certainly a great basketball player, class of 1958
14. McCreery, Gene, a life long leader and educator, class of 1930
15. Murphy, Bob, a life long friend and teammate, class of 1958
16. Murphy, John, a life long friend and outstanding basketball player, class of 1959
17. Pitzer, Mark, a life long friend and teammate, class of 1958
18. Ramsey, John, a life long friend and outstanding teammate and basketball player, class of 1958
19. Wray, John, the best brother you can have, an outstanding athlete, coach and Athletic Director, member of the Delaware County Athletic Hall of Fame, class of 1956
20. Wray, Donald "Rudy", great brother, hard worker, and inspiration, class of 1961
21. Yeager, Helen (Finley), one of the supporting rocks of the Yeager brothers, wife of Bill, class of 1935

Sources

1. Black, Jim. The History of the Delaware County Basketball Tournament. Muncie, Indiana. Delaware Litho, Inc. 1977
2. Hinshaw, Gregory P. Harrison and Washington Local History Resources for Harrison and Washington Townships. Delaware County, Indiana. 1998
3. Hoover, Dwight W. Middletown Revisited. Muncie, Indiana. Ball State University, 1990
4. Hoover, Dwight W. and Rodman, Jane. A Pictorial History of Indiana. Bloomington, Indiana. Indiana University Press. 1980
5. Lynd, Robert S. and Lynd, Helen Merrell, Middletown. San Diego New York London. Harcourt Brace and Company. 1929 and 1957
6. Lynd, Robert S. and Lynd, Helen Merrell, Middletown in Transition. New York and London. Harcourt Brace Jovanovich, Publishers. 1937 and 1965
7. Muncie Star. Resourced from the 1950's Archives at the Muncie, Indiana, Public Library.
8. Muncie Press. Resourced from the 1950's Archives at the Muncie, Indiana, Public Library
9. Stodghill, Dick and Stodghill, Jackie. Bearcats! A History of Basketball at Muncie Central High School. Muncie, Indiana. JLT Publications. 1988
10. Wray, John. Statistical Data. Muncie, Indiana. Unpublished, 1950's

Index

D

E

F

L

M

N

O

P

R

S

T

U

V

W

Y

About the Author

Harrison Hunt grew up in Delaware County, Indiana, during the 1950's. He was a high school athlete when athletics were the social focus of every small school society.

Mr. Hunt is a graduate of Ball State University and holds a MBA degree from Butler University in Indianapolis, Indiana. His professional life has included being a business executive, college professor, consultant and entrepreneur. He has resided in Indianapolis, the Twin cities in Minnesota, New York and the Gulf Coast of Florida. He now resides near Dale Hollow Lake very close to Byrdstown, Tennessee.

He is now semi-retired and is a writer focused on novels.

LaVergne, TN USA
12 May 2010

182522LV00002B/7/A

9 781434 309013